Good Housekeeping Cookery Club

COOKBOOK

Good Housekeeping Cookery Club

COOKBOOK

Recipes for family meals, quick suppers and entertaining

EBURY PRESS
LONDON

First published in the United Kingdom in 1997 by Ebury Press
Random House, 20 Vauxhall Bridge Road,
London, SW1V 2SA

Random House Australia (Pty) Limited
20 Alfred Street, Milsons Point, Sydney,
New South Wales, 2061 Australia

Random House New Zealand Limited
18 Poland Road, Glenfield,
Auckland 10, New Zealand

Random House South Africa (Pty) Limited
Endulini, Jubilee Road, Parktown 2193, South Africa

Random House UK Limited Reg. No. 954009

A catalogue record of this book is available from the British
Library

ISBN 0 09 185255 2

Managing Editor: JANET ILLSLEY
Design: SARA KIDD
Photography: KARL ADAMSON, LAURIE EVANS, KEN FIELD,
GUS FILGATE, GRAHAM KIRK, JAMES MURPHY

Printed and bound in Italy by New Interlitho Italia S.p.a.

The material in this book was previously
published in *Good Housekeeping Cookery Club Collection*.

CONTENTS

COOKERY NOTES

- Both metric and imperial measures are given for the recipes. Follow *either* metric or imperial throughout.
- All spoon measures are level unless otherwise stated. Sets of measuring spoons are available in metric and imperial for accurate measurement of small quantities.
- Ovens should be preheated to the specified temperature. Grills should also be preheated. The cooking times given in the recipes assume that this has been done.
- Where a stage is specified under freezing instructions, the dish should be frozen at the end of that stage.
- Size 2 eggs should be used unless otherwise specified.

SOUPS AND STARTERS

GARLIC, BEAN AND TOMATO SOUP WITH PESTO

This is a soup confirmed garlic lovers – a caramelised garlic broth forms the basis of the stock, and a garlic pesto sauce is served as a garnish. Caramelising raw garlic changes its character dramatically, giving it a far sweeter and milder flavour. Cooking it in this way also makes garlic more digestible.

SERVES 4

125 g (4 oz) dried borlotti
  beans, soaked overnight in
  cold water (see note)
1.2 litres (2 pints) vegetable
  stock
1 head of garlic
30 ml (2 tbsp) olive oil
450 g (1 lb) ripe tomatoes
15 ml (1 tbsp) lemon juice
salt and pepper
PESTO
1 garlic clove chopped
2.5 ml (½ tsp) sea salt
25 g (1 oz) basil leaves
25 g (1 oz) pine nuts
125 ml (4 fl oz) extra-virgin
  olive oil
30 ml (2 tbsp) freshly grated
  Parmesan cheese

PREPARATION TIME
15 minutes, plus overnight
soaking
COOKING TIME
1 hour
FREEZING
Suitable: Without the pesto

530 CALS PER SERVING

1. Preheat the oven to 200°C (400°F), Mark 6. Drain and rinse the beans and place in a saucepan with the stock. Bring to the boil and boil rapidly for 10 minutes. Reduce the heat, cover and simmer for 40-45 minutes until the beans are tender.

2. Meanwhile, separate and peel the garlic cloves. Place them in a roasting tin, drizzle with the oil and bake near the top of the oven for 15 minutes. Meanwhile, roughly chop the tomatoes. Add to the garlic, stir to mix and bake for a further 10-15 minutes until the garlic is lightly browned and the tomatoes are soft. Set aside.

3. Transfer the cooked beans and their liquid to a blender or food processor, then add the tomato and garlic mixture, salt and pepper. Purée until fairly smooth, then return to the pan. Add the lemon juice and check the seasoning. Heat through for 5 minutes.

4. Meanwhile, make the pesto. Place the garlic, salt, basil and pine nuts in a food processor and blend until fairly smooth. Gradually blend in the oil. Stir in the cheese and salt and pepper to taste.

5. Ladle the soup into warmed bowls and top each serving with a spoonful of pesto.

NOTE: To save time, use a 400 g (14 oz) can borlotti or haricot beans rather than dried beans and reduce the stock to 900 ml (1½ pints). Rinse the beans before puréeing them with the stock and tomato mixture in step 3.

VARIATIONS

Add 225 g (8 oz) button mushrooms to the tomato and garlic mixture with an extra 15 ml (1 tbsp) olive oil. Bake as above, stir into the cooked beans and add 125 g (4 oz) each of peas, broad beans and diced broccoli. Cook until tender and serve topped with the pesto.

TECHNIQUE

Bake the garlic and tomatoes until soft and lightly browned.

Spicy Parsnip and Carrot Soup with Cumin

A wonderfully warming vegetarian soup, with a delicious hint of spicy cumin seeds. As the parsnip and carrot purée is sufficient to thicken the soup, there are no added calories in the form of flour – making it an ideal recipe for slimmers. For optimum flavour, use homemade vegetable stock. Serve the soup as a sustaining lunch, accompanied by wholemeal bread or crusty rolls.

SERVES 4

1 onion
450 g (1 lb) parsnips
225 g (8 oz) carrots
30 ml (2 tbsp) olive oil
15 ml (1 tbsp) curry powder
350 ml (³⁄₄ pint) vegetable
   stock
300 ml (¹⁄₂ pint) semi-
   skimmed milk
salt and pepper
TO GARNISH
10 ml (2 tsp) cumin seeds

PREPARATION TIME
15 minutes
COOKING TIME
15-20 minutes
FREEZING
Suitable

200 CALS PER SERVING

1. Peel and finely chop the onion. Peel the parsnips, cut in half and remove the woody stems. Peel the carrots. Cut the parsnips and carrots into even-sized pieces.

2. Heat the olive oil in a heavy-based saucepan, add the vegetables and stir to lightly coat in the oil. Cover and cook for a few minutes until the vegetables are slightly softened. Sprinkle in the curry powder and cook, stirring, for 1 minute.

3. Stir in the vegetable stock and milk, and season with salt and pepper. Bring to the boil, then reduce the heat to a gentle simmer and cook for 15-20 minutes until the vegetables are soft.

4. Allow the soup to cool a little, then transfer to a blender or food processor and work until smooth. If the consistency is a little too thick for your liking, add a dash more milk or vegetable stock.

5. Toast the cumin seeds by gently frying them in a non-stick pan, or spread on a baking sheet and grill under a medium heat. Meanwhile, return the soup to the saucepan and reheat gently. Serve the soup in warmed soup bowls, garnished with a sprinkling of cumin seeds.

VARIATIONS

Use pumpkin in place of carrots for a vibrant soup with an excellent flavour. Alternatively, use a mixture of root vegetables, such as swede, parsnip and potato.

TECHNIQUE

Purée the soup in a blender or food processor, then return to the saucepan and reheat gently.

JERUSALEM ARTICHOKE AND PARMESAN SOUP

An unusual combination of mild Jerusalem artichokes with a hint of spice and the nutty taste of Parmesan cheese. The flavour of fresh Parmesan makes this soup really special. Don't be tempted to use the dry cheese sold in cartons – it bears no comparison to the real thing!

450 g (1 lb) Jerusalem artichokes
2 shallots
50 g (2 oz) butter
5 ml (1 tsp) mild curry paste
900 ml (1½ pints) chicken or vegetable stock
150 ml (¼ pint) single cream (or milk for a less rich soup)
freshly grated nutmeg, to taste
pinch of cayenne pepper
60 ml (4 tbsp) freshly grated Parmesan cheese
salt and pepper
MELBA TOAST
3-4 slices day-old softgrain white bread
a little freshly grated Parmesan cheese, for sprinkling
1.25 ml (¼ tsp) paprika

PREPARATION TIME
15 minutes
COOKING TIME
25 minutes
FREEZING
Suitable

1. Scrub the Jerusalem artichokes thoroughly to remove any dirt. Pat dry, then slice thinly. Peel and dice the shallots.

2. Melt the butter in a large saucepan and add the shallots. Cook gently for 5 minutes until soft and golden. Stir in the curry paste and cook for 1 minute. Add the sliced artichokes and stock; stir well. Bring to the boil, cover and simmer for about 15 minutes or until the artichokes are tender.

3. Meanwhile, make the Melba toast. Preheat the oven to 180°C (350°F) Mark 4. Toast the bread lightly on both sides. Quickly cut off the crusts and split each slice in two. Scrape off any doughy bits, then sprinkle with Parmesan and paprika. Place on a baking sheet and bake in the oven for 10-15 minutes or until uniformly golden.

4. Add the cream, nutmeg and cayenne to the soup. Transfer to a blender or food processor and work until smooth, then pass through a sieve into a clean saucepan. Reheat the soup and stir in the Parmesan cheese. Taste and adjust the seasoning. Serve at once, with the hot Melba toast.

NOTE: If preferred the Melba toast can be prepared ahead, allowed to cool, then stored in an airtight tin. Warm through in the oven before serving.

VARIATION

Replace the Jerusalem artichokes with 1 large cauliflower. Cut away the leaves and core, and discard. Divide the cauliflower into florets. Add to the shallots with the stock and bring to the boil. Simmer for about 10 minutes or until very soft, then continue as in step 4.

TECHNIQUE

To make the Melba toast, carefully split each slice of toast horizontally in two. On baking these fine slices will curl.

GRILLED PEPPER AND AUBERGINE SOUP

Peppers and aubergine become sweet as their flesh caramelises under the grill, giving this soup an intensity of flavour that is hard to surpass. The saffron cream garnish is similar to *rouille*.

SERVES 4-6

2 large red peppers

1 large aubergine

90 ml (3 fl oz) olive oil

1 large onion

2 garlic cloves

5 ml (1 tsp) grated lemon
   rind

15 ml (1 tbsp) chopped fresh
   thyme

5 ml (1 tsp) dried oregano

400 g (14 oz) can chopped
   tomatoes

900 ml (1½ pints) vegetable
   or chicken stock

1 bay leaf

30 ml (2 tbsp) chopped fresh
   basil

salt and pepper

SAFFRON CREAM

small pinch of saffron strands

1 egg yolk

1 garlic clove, crushed

2.5 ml (½ tsp) cayenne
   pepper

10 ml (2 tsp) lemon juice

150-175 ml (5-6 fl oz) olive oil

PREPARATION TIME
25 minutes
COOKING TIME
45-50 minutes
FREEZING
Suitable: Without saffron cream

390-300 CALS PER SERVING

1. Preheat the grill. Quarter, core and deseed the red peppers. Brush with a little olive oil and grill for 3-4 minutes on each side until charred and tender. Transfer to a plate, cover with a cloth and leave until cool enough to handle. Peel the peppers and roughly chop the flesh.

2. Thinly slice the aubergine lengthways. Brush with oil and grill for 4-5 minutes on each side until charred and tender. Leave until cool enough to handle, then chop roughly.

3. Peel and chop the onion and garlic. Heat the remaining oil in a large pan, add the onion, garlic, lemon rind, thyme and oregano and fry, stirring, for 10 minutes until browned. Add the peppers, aubergine, tomatoes, stock and bay leaf. Bring to the boil, cover and simmer for 20 minutes. Discard the bay leaf.

4. Meanwhile, make the saffron cream. Put the saffron in a small bowl, pour on 15 ml (1 tbsp) boiling water and leave to soak for 5 minutes. In a bowl, whisk the egg yolk with the garlic, cayenne, lemon juice and seasoning until pale and slightly thickened. Gradually whisk in the oil, until thick. Stir in the saffron liquid and seasoning to taste.

5. Transfer the soup to a blender or food processor. Add the basil and work

until smooth. Return to the pan and heat through. Adjust the seasoning and pour into warmed soup bowls. Spoon a little saffron cream onto each portion, garnish with basil leaves and serve at once.

VARIATION

Replace the aubergine with 2 yellow peppers and grill as above. Divide all other ingredients in half and cook in separate pans, adding the red peppers to one and the yellow peppers to the other. Cook until tender and purée separately to give two different coloured pepper soups. Serve half and half in each bowl, swirling them attractively, and garnish with saffron cream.

TECHNIQUE

For the saffron cream, whisk in the oil a little at a time, beating well between each addition.

MARINATED PEPPERS WITH ARTICHOKES AND ANCHOVIES

There is nothing more evocative of sunny, warm Mediterranean meals than sweet roasted red peppers marinated in golden, garlicky olive oil with artichoke hearts and anchovies to add extra bite. Left overnight for the flavours to mature, the peppers release a sweet juice into the oil, making a delicious sauce – perfect for mopping up with copious amounts of bread.

SERVES 6

6 red, orange or yellow
   peppers (or a mixture)
12 artichoke hearts in oil,
   drained
24 salted anchovies (see
   below), or canned
   anchovy fillets
salt and pepper
4 garlic cloves
30 ml (2 tbsp) chopped fresh
   oregano
extra-virgin olive oil, for
   marinating

PREPARATION TIME
20 minutes, plus overnight
marinating
COOKING TIME
10-15 minutes
FREEZING
Not suitable

300 CALS PER SERVING

1. Preheat the grill to high. Place the whole peppers in the grill pan and grill, turning occasionally, until the skins are evenly charred all over. Place in a covered bowl for 1-2 minutes until cool enough to handle.

2. Slip off the skins while the peppers are still warm, then cut in half lengthways and scrape out the seeds. Place the peppers cut-side up in a shallow dish.

3. Cut the artichoke hearts in half and place two halves in each pepper half. Lay the anchovy fillets on top. Season well with salt and pepper. Peel and slice the garlic. Scatter the garlic and chopped oregano over the peppers.

4. Pour over enough olive oil to cover the peppers (see note). Cover the dish and leave to marinate in the refrigerator overnight to permit the flavours to blend. Allow to come to room temperature before serving, with crusty Italian bread.

NOTE: Use the leftover flavoured olive oil again and again to make more of the same dish, or in salad dressings.

SALTED ANCHOVIES: These have a much better flavour than canned anchovy fillets. They are available in jars from Italian delicatessens and larger supermarkets. Usually salted anchovies are whole and have to be rinsed, split open and the backbone and other small bones removed.

VARIATION

Fill the peppers with grilled lengthwise slices of courgette and top with cubed mozzarella cheese.

TECHNIQUE

Place two artichoke halves in each grilled pepper half. Top with the anchovy fillets.

GRILLED TOMATO AND MOZZARELLA SALAD

This hot salad starter can be prepared ahead, chilled, then grilled just before serving. Make sure you use tomatoes which are ripe and have plenty of flavour – it does make a difference. If you are buying from a supermarket, look for the packs marked 'grown for flavour'.

SERVES 4

175 g (6 oz) aubergine
45 ml (3 tbsp) olive oil
450 g (1 lb) tomatoes
150 g (5 oz) mozzarella
    cheese
60 ml (4 tbsp) torn fresh
    basil leaves
finely grated rind of 1 lemon
5 ml (1 tsp) lemon juice
salt and pepper
TO GARNISH
basil leaves

PREPARATION TIME
10 minutes
COOKING TIME
About 10 minutes
FREEZING
Not suitable

240 CALS PER SERVING

1. Preheat the grill. Cut the aubergine into thin slices. Brush very lightly with some of the olive oil and place on the grill rack. Grill the aubergine slices on both sides until they are crisp and golden brown; do not let them turn too dark at this stage.

2. Thinly slice the tomatoes. Cut the mozzarella cheese into thin slices.

3. In a bowl, whisk together the remaining olive oil, torn basil, lemon rind and juice. Season with salt and pepper.

4. Arrange the tomato, aubergine and mozzarella slices, overlapping in a single layer, in a large shallow flameproof dish. Spoon the dressing evenly over the top.

5. Place under a hot grill for 3-4 minutes or until the mozzarella begins to melt. Sprinkle with salt and pepper and garnish with basil leaves. Serve immediately, accompanied by warm crusty bread.

VARIATION

Instead of basil, flavour the salad with 45 ml (3 tbsp) snipped chives or chopped coriander leaves.

TECHNIQUE

Layer the aubergine, tomato and mozzarella slices in the dish, overlapping them.

ROASTED VEGETABLES IN GARLIC BREAD BASKETS

Wholemeal bread baskets are rubbed with garlic, baked until crisp, then filled with a selection of roasted Mediterranean vegetables to delicious effect. Drizzling the baskets with a little balsamic vinegar lifts the flavour and a pretty garnish of basil and black olive slivers adds the finishing touch. An attractive starter to complement any meal.

SERVES 6

2 red onions
2 garlic cloves, peeled
1 yellow pepper
1 red pepper
1 small aubergine
2 courgettes
15 ml (1 tbsp) olive oil
pinch of sea salt
4 fresh rosemary sprigs
12 slices wholemeal bread
15 ml (1 tbsp) black olive
  paste
15 ml (1 tbsp) balsamic
  vinegar
TO GARNISH
12 basil sprigs
few black olives, stoned and
  sliced

PREPARATION TIME
30 minutes
COOKING TIME
20-30 minutes
FREEZING
Not suitable

215 CALS PER SERVING

1. Preheat the oven to 230°C (450°F) Mark 8. Peel the onions and slice lengthwise. Halve one of the garlic cloves and set aside; crush the other garlic clove. Halve the peppers, then remove the core and seeds. Cut the peppers, aubergine and courgettes into 2.5 cm (1 inch) chunks.

2. Place all the vegetables in a roasting tin, drizzle over the olive oil and sprinkle with the sea salt, rosemary and crushed garlic. Bake in the oven for 20-30 minutes, turning occasionally until just tinged brown at the edges.

3. Remove the crusts from the bread and roll out each slice lightly. Cut a 9 cm (3½ inch) circle from each slice using a plain cutter, and rub with the halved garlic clove. Line a 12-hole deep bun tin or muffin tin with the bread rounds.

4. Place in the oven for 5 minutes. Carefully remove the bread baskets from the tin and return to the oven for 5 minutes to allow the bread to crisp.

5. Spread a little olive paste over the base of each basket. Remove the roasted vegetables from the oven and divide between the toasted bread baskets. Just before serving, drizzle a little balsamic

vinegar over each basket. Garnish with sprigs of basil and slivers of black olive. Serve warm.

VARIATIONS

Use the bread baskets as containers for other combinations of vegetables, such as lightly roasted leeks, courgettes and cauliflower.

> **TECHNIQUE**

To shape the bread baskets, line a 12-hole deep bun tin with the bread slices.

MUSHROOM PÂTÉ WITH MADEIRA

This is a rich mushroom pâté, flavoured with dried porcini and a variety of fresh mushrooms. You can use any combination of mushrooms, but try to include some flavourful wild ones or cultivated dark field mushrooms. Don't be tempted to use all button mushrooms as the end result will lack colour and flavour. Serve the pâté with hot olive bread, ciabatta, French bread or toast.

SERVES 6

15 g (½ oz) dried porcini
   mushrooms (see note)
150 ml (¼ pint) milk
1 small onion
1 garlic clove (optional)
25 g (1 oz) butter
coarse sea salt and pepper
350 g (12 oz) mushrooms
125 g (4 oz) ricotta cheese
15 ml (1 tbsp) Madeira
2.5 ml (½ tsp) balsamic
   vinegar or lemon juice
5 ml (1 tsp) mushroom
   ketchup
freshly grated nutmeg, to
   taste
15-30 ml (1-2 tbsp) chopped
   fresh parsley or coriander
   (optional)
TO GARNISH
chopped parsley or
   coriander

PREPARATION TIME
15 minutes, plus soaking
COOKING TIME
20-25 minutes
FREEZING
Not suitable

100 CALS PER SERVING

1. Rinse the porcini under cold running water to wash away the grit, then place in a bowl. Pour on the warm milk and leave to soak for 20 minutes. Drain the porcini and chop finely.

2. Peel and finely chop the onion and garlic, if using. Melt the butter in a saucepan, add the onion and garlic and fry gently for 5-10 minutes until softened and transparent. Season with salt and pepper.

3. Meanwhile, wipe the fresh mushrooms with a damp cloth to clean them, then chop finely.

4. Add the porcini and fresh mushrooms to the onion and garlic, increase the heat a little and cook, stirring occasionally, for about 15 minutes until the mushrooms are tender and reduced to a thick pulp. Leave to cool slightly.

5. Transfer the mushroom mixture to a food processor or bowl. Add the ricotta, Madeira, balsamic vinegar, mushroom ketchup and nutmeg and process very briefly or stir until evenly mixed; the pâté should retain a coarse texture. Stir in the chopped parsley or coriander if using. Adjust the seasoning.

6. Turn into a serving dish or individual ramekins and garnish with parsley or coriander. Serve with olive bread, ciabatta, French bread or toast.

NOTE: If dried porcini are unobtainable, use an extra 125 g (4 oz) flavourful fresh mushrooms.

TECHNIQUE

Rinse the porcini under cold running water to wash away the grit.

FISH AND SHELLFISH

SALMON EN PAPILLOTE WITH LIME BUTTER SAUCE

Salmon steaks – scented with lime and ginger – are gently cooked in paper parcels, then served with a rich butter sauce flavoured with lime and dry sherry. The sauce can be made in advance and gently reheated in a bain-marie as the fish is cooking, making this recipe a perfect dinner party dish.

SERVES 4

75 g (3 oz) unsalted butter

2 limes

15 g (½ oz) fresh root
  ginger

4 salmon steaks, each about
  175 g (6 oz)

salt and pepper

4 spring onions, trimmed

pinch of sugar

45 ml (3 tbsp) dry sherry
  (preferably Manzanilla)

45 ml (3 tbsp) double cream

PREPARATION TIME
20 minutes
COOKING TIME
12-15 minutes
FREEZING
Not suitable

635 CALS PER SERVING

1. Preheat the oven to 200°C (400°F) Mark 6. Cut 4 baking parchment or greaseproof paper rectangles, measuring 30 x 20 cm (12 x 8 inches). Using 25 g (1 oz) of the butter, grease the paper.

2. Grate the rind from 1 lime and squeeze the juice. Peel the ginger, then cut into very fine slices or julienne strips.

3. Place a salmon steak on one half of each paper rectangle. Season with salt and pepper. Scatter the lime rind and ginger on top, then sprinkle with the lime juice. Fold the other half of the paper over the top, brushing the edges together. Make small overlapping folds along the edges to seal. Place on a baking sheet and set aside.

4. To make the sauce, chop the spring onions. Heat 15 g (½ oz) butter in a small pan, add the spring onions and cook until softened. Squeeze the juice from the remaining lime. Add to the onions with the sugar and sherry. Increase the heat and boil steadily until the liquid is reduced by half.

5. Place the fish papillotes in the oven and cook for 12-15 minutes; the parcels will puff up.

6. Add the cream to the sauce and allow to bubble for a few seconds. Gradually whisk in the remaining butter, a piece at a time, taking the pan off the heat occasionally to prevent the sauce from splitting. The sauce should be smooth and slightly thickened. Season with salt and pepper.

7. Serve the papillotes at the table, allowing each person to enjoy the fragrance as they open their own parcel. Serve the sauce separately.

NOTE: Manzanilla sherry has a dry, almost salty tang which complements the fish well. If unavailable, fino sherry could be used instead.

TECHNIQUE

Fold the paper to enclose the salmon steak, bringing the edges together, then seal.

TROUT WITH DILL AND HORSERADISH MAYONNAISE

Each pink-fleshed trout lies on a long leaf of Cos lettuce, making a simple, elegant dish – perfect for a supper party. The cooking is beautifully simple too, for the fish complete their cooking in the cooling poaching liquor. Serve with a potato salad, ideally in a hazelnut oil dressing and finished with a scattering of nuts.

SERVES 4

4 gutted trout, each about
   200 g (7 oz)
100 ml (3½ fl oz) white wine
   vinegar
10 ml (2 tsp) black
   peppercorns
10 ml (2 tsp) dill seeds
   (optional)
3 bay leaves
5 ml (1 tsp) salt
MAYONNAISE
1 Bramley apple, about
   150 g (5 oz)
150 ml (¼ pint) good-quality
   mayonnaise
45 ml (3 tbsp) chopped fresh
   dill leaves
10 ml (2 tsp) grated
   horseradish or
   horseradish sauce
TO SERVE
8 long Cos lettuce leaves
dill sprigs, bay leaves and
   lime wedges, to garnish

PREPARATION TIME
15 minutes
COOKING TIME
35-40 minutes, including cooling
FREEZING
Not suitable

560 CALS PER SERVING

1. Wash the fish inside and out under cold running water. Fill a large roasting tin with boiling water. Add the wine vinegar, peppercorns, dill seeds if using, bay leaves and salt. Immerse the fish in the liquid and bring back to the boil. As soon as it reaches the boil, turn off the heat and leave the fish undisturbed in the liquid for at least 20 minutes.

2. For the mayonnaise, peel, quarter, core and slice the apple. Place in a small pan with 45 ml (3 tbsp) water. Cover and cook until the apple is softened to a purée. Beat until smooth and allow to cool, then mix with the mayonnaise, chopped dill and horseradish.

3. Lift the trout from the poaching liquor, remove the skin, and their heads if preferred. Lay each fish in a long lettuce leaf on a serving plate and spoon some of the dill and apple mayonnaise alongside. Garnish with dill sprigs, bay leaves and lime wedges.

NOTE: Trout are often sold ready-gutted, but if they are whole allow a little extra weight and ask the fishmonger to gut them for you.

VARIATION

Use the same poaching method for a whole salmon, bringing to the boil then leaving to cool in the liquor, but put the salmon into *cold* seasoned water and raise the liquid to boiling point slowly.

TECHNIQUE

Carefully remove the skin from each trout to reveal the pink flesh.

FRIED SKATE WINGS WITH OLIVE AND HERB SAUCE

Skate wings have a wonderful texture and are surprisingly easy to eat, as the flesh just falls away from the bones. This is a relatively quick and easy dish, although you may need two frying pans to cook the fish. Serve with boiled new potatoes and lightly cooked fresh spinach.

SERVES 4

4 skate wings, each
   300-350 g (10-12 oz)
salt and pepper
60 ml (4 tbsp) plain flour
50 g (2 oz) butter
30 ml (2 tbsp) oil
SAUCE
2 garlic cloves
8 anchovy fillets
30 ml (2 tbsp) capers,
   drained and rinsed
10 ml (2 tsp) black olive
   paste
15 ml (1 tbsp) sun-dried
   tomato paste
60 ml (4 tbsp) chopped
   fresh parsley
15 ml (1 tbsp) chopped
   fresh chives
60 ml (4 tbsp) extra-virgin
   olive oil
juice of 1 lemon
TO GARNISH
few chives

PREPARATION TIME
10 minutes
COOKING TIME
12 minutes
FREEZING
Not suitable

600 CALS PER SERVING

1. First make the sauce. Crush the garlic cloves and place in a bowl. Drain the anchovy fillets on kitchen paper, chop finely and add to the garlic. Add the capers, olive paste, sun-dried tomato paste, parsley, chives, olive oil and lemon juice. Mix thoroughly.

2. If the skate wings are very large, cut them into more manageable pieces. Season with salt and pepper and dust with flour.

3. Heat the butter and oil in a very large frying pan, or two smaller ones. When the butter begins to foam, add the skate wings and fry gently for about 5 minutes on each side or until just cooked. To test, prise a little of the flesh away from the bone with the tip of a knife: if it comes away easily the fish is cooked.

4. Pour the sauce around the fish and heat through for 1-2 minutes. Serve immediately, garnished with chives.

NOTE: Both olive and sun-dried tomato pastes are available from larger supermarkets and good delicatessens. If unavailable, or if you prefer a coarse textured sauce, use chopped pitted olives and sun-dried tomatoes instead.

TECHNIQUE

To check if the fish is cooked, prise a little of the flesh away from the bone with the tip of a knife. If it comes away easily the skate is cooked.

GRILLED PLAICE WITH RED PEPPER SALSA

Plaice is a good value fish to use, but often forgotten in place of more exotic species. Served like this – on a split pea purée with a red pepper salsa – it makes an unusual and tasty dish.

SERVES 4

125 g (4 oz) split yellow peas

1 onion

2 garlic cloves, crushed

1 bay leaf

6 fresh thyme sprigs

salt and pepper

30 ml (2 tbsp) plain flour

45 ml (3 tbsp) finely
   chopped fresh parsley

4 plaice fillets

15-30 ml (1-2 tbsp) olive oil

SALSA

1 red pepper

1 plum tomato

½ red onion

2.5 ml (½ tsp) mustard
   seeds

pinch of sugar

TO GARNISH

watercress sprigs

PREPARATION TIME
10 minutes
COOKING TIME
40-45 minutes
FREEZING
Not suitable

390 CALS PER SERVING

1. Rinse the split yellow peas in a sieve under running cold water, then place in a saucepan.

2. Peel and finely chop the onion and add to the split peas with the garlic, herbs and seasoning. Pour on 450 ml (¾ pint) cold water, bring to the boil, then simmer for 35-40 minutes, until soft and mushy. Drain, and remove the herb sprigs. Check the seasoning and beat to form a rough-textured purée.

3. Meanwhile, prepare the salsa. Place the pepper under a preheated hot grill and cook, turning, until blackened. Cover with a damp tea-towel and leave until cool enough to handle, then remove the skin. Cut the pepper in half and remove the core and seeds. Finely dice the pepper and place in a small bowl. Finely dice the tomato. Peel and finely chop the onion. Add the tomato and onion to the red pepper with the mustard seeds and sugar. Stir well and set aside.

4. Preheat the grill to medium. Season the flour with salt and pepper and mix in the parsley. Dip the flesh side of each plaice fillet in the mixture to coat evenly, then lay skin-side down on the grill rack. Drizzle each fillet with about 1.25 ml (¼ tsp) of the olive oil. Grill for about 5 minutes, depending on the thickness

of the fillets, until the flesh turns white and is just firm to the touch.

5. To serve, place a spoonful of the split pea mixture on each warmed serving plate. Lay a fish fillet on top and spoon over 2-3 teaspoons of the salsa. Garnish with watercress.

VARIATION

Replace the plaice fillets with lemon sole fillets. Replace the grilled pepper with tomato.

TECHNIQUE

Dip the flesh side of each plaice fillet in the flour mixture to coat evenly.

ROASTED MONKFISH TAILS WITH ROCKET PESTO ON A BED OF SHALLOTS

A wonderfully tender and flavoursome fish dish. Roasting the fish at a high temperature ensures it cooks quickly and is succulent. Rocket gives the pesto a good flavour as well as an intense green colour.

SERVES 4

225 g (8 oz) shallots
4 garlic cloves (unpeeled)
30 ml (2 tbsp) cider vinegar
30 ml (2 tbsp) olive oil
900 g (2 lb) monkfish tails (on the bone)
salt and pepper
4 fresh rosemary sprigs
4 fresh thyme sprigs
4 fresh oregano sprigs
ROCKET PESTO
50 g (2 oz) rocket leaves
15 g ($\frac{1}{2}$ oz) fresh Parmesan cheese
15 ml (1 tbsp) olive oil
30 ml (2 tbsp) apple juice

PREPARATION TIME
30 minutes
COOKING TIME
35-45 minutes
FREEZING
Not suitable

320 CALS PER SERVING

1. Preheat the oven to 220°C (425°F) Mark 7. Peel the shallots and cut in half. Place in a roasting pan with the garlic, sprinkle with the cider vinegar and oil and cook for 15-20 minutes.

2. Meanwhile, make the pesto. Wash the rocket, removing any bruised leaves. Place in a blender or food processor. Grate the Parmesan cheese and add to the blender with the oil. With the machine running, pour the apple juice through the feeder tube in a steady stream. Blend until a smooth paste is formed.

3. Remove any skin and membrane from the monkfish: cut around the membrane, pull back and tear off using your fingers.

4. Cut along one side of the centre bone, as close to the bone as possible, and remove the fillet. Repeat on the other side.

5. Lay one fillet, cut side up, on a board and spread with the pesto. Place the other fillet on top, cut side down, to sandwich the pesto. Tie the two pieces together at regular intervals with string.

6. Remove the roasting pan from the oven, push the shallots and garlic to the

sides, and lay the monkfish parcel in the centre of the pan. Sprinkle with salt and pepper and add the herb sprigs. Cook for 20-25 minutes, until the monkfish turns opaque.

7. To serve, remove the string and lift the fish onto a serving platter, discarding any milky residue. Place the shallots and garlic around the fish. Serve with boiled new potatoes or simmered wild rice and steamed mangetouts.

VARIATION

Use a tail end of salmon instead of monkfish. For speed, use ready-made pesto.

TECHNIQUE

To fillet the fish, cut along both sides of the central bone, placing the knife as close as possible to the bone.

BRAISED COD BOULANGÈRE

Thick cod fillets are pan-fried briefly to give them a golden hue, then baked on a bed of sliced potatoes and onions, flavoured with herbs and moistened with stock. This is the perfect supper dish – easy to prepare and cook, and can be brought to the table in the dish it's cooked in. Serve with a green vegetable; fresh peas, when in season, are the perfect accompaniment.

SERVES 4

700 g (1½ lb) potatoes
1 onion
75 g (3 oz) butter
salt and pepper
few fresh thyme sprigs
300 ml (½ pint) chicken
   stock
4 thick cod fillets, each
   about 150 g (5 oz)
snipped chives, to garnish

PREPARATION TIME
10 minutes
COOKING TIME
1 hour
FREEZING
Not suitable

395 CALS PER SERVING

1. Preheat the oven to 190°C (375°F) Mark 5. Peel the potatoes and onion, then slice both thinly and as evenly as possible.

2. Use 25 g (1 oz) of the butter to grease an ovenproof dish. Layer the potatoes and onion alternately in the dish, sprinkling each layer with salt, pepper and thyme. Dot with half of the remaining butter. Pour in the stock and bake in the oven for 40-50 minutes.

3. Melt the remaining butter in a non-stick frying pan, add the cod fillets and fry briefly until golden on both sides.

4. Place the fish on top of the potatoes. Cover the dish and return to the oven for a further 10-15 minutes. The fish should be firm, but tender; check by prising the flesh away from the bone – if it comes away easily, the fish is ready.

5. Sprinkle the dish with the chives and serve immediately.

VARIATION

Use fillets of haddock, sole or whiting instead of cod.

TECHNIQUE

Layer the potatoes and onions in a greased ovenproof dish, sprinkling each layer with salt, pepper and thyme.

PRAWNS FRIED WITH GREENS

This is a good way to use those interesting greens sold in Chinese food stores. Pak choi is the one with the long, ribbed white stalks and dark green leaves which grow from a central root, rather like a head of celery. Baby pak choi – the mini variety – is good in this dish as it can be left whole for maximum visual impact. Chinese flowering cabbage has thin white stems, bright green leaves and tiny yellow flowers. Some supermarkets now stock Dutch-grown varieties of these Chinese vegetables.

SERVES 4-6

2 garlic cloves

1 lemon grass stalk

2 kaffir lime leaves

2 red shallots, or 1 small red onion

1-2 hot red chillies

4 cm (1½ inch) piece fresh root ginger

15 ml (1 tbsp) coriander seeds

75 g (3 oz) green beans

175 g (6 oz) mangetouts

450 g (1 lb) large raw prawns (see note)

1 small head of pak choi or Chinese flowering cabbage, or 2-3 baby pak choi (or a mixture)

30 ml (2 tbsp) vegetable oil

juice of 1 lime, or to taste

30 ml (2 tbsp) nam pla (Thai fish sauce)

lime halves, to garnish

PREPARATION TIME
20 minutes
COOKING TIME
About 10 minutes
FREEZING
Not suitable

195-130 CALS PER SERVING

1. Peel the garlic and slice thinly. Cut the lemon grass in half and bruise with a rolling pin. Tear the kaffir lime leaves into small pieces. Peel and thinly slice the shallots or onion. Slice the chillies, discarding the seeds if a milder flavour is preferred. Peel the ginger and cut into long, thin shreds. Crush the coriander seeds. Trim the beans and mangetouts.

2. Peel the prawns, leaving the tail end attached. Using a small sharp knife, make a shallow slit along the outer curve from the tail to the head end and remove the dark intestinal vein. Rinse under cold running water, drain and pat dry with kitchen paper.

3. Trim the pak choi or Chinese flowering cabbage, removing any discoloured leaves or damaged stems. Leave baby pak choi whole; tear other leaves into manageable pieces.

4. Heat the oil in a wok or large frying pan. Add the garlic, lemon grass, lime leaves, shallots, chillies, ginger and coriander seeds, and stir-fry for 2 minutes. Add the green beans and cook for 2 minutes. Add the prawns, mangetouts and pak choi or Chinese flowering cabbage and stir-fry for 2-3 minutes, until the vegetables are cooked but still crisp and the prawns are pink and opaque.

5. Add the nam pla and lime juice, and heat through for 1 minute. Serve immediately, while the vegetables are crisp.

NOTE: If raw prawns are unobtainable, use cooked ones instead. Add with the lime juice; heat through for 1 minute only.

VARIATION

Replace the prawns with skinned chicken breast fillets, cut into wafer-thin slices. Stir-fry with the beans at stage 4.

TECHNIQUE

Using a small sharp knife, make a shallow slit along the outer curve of each prawn from tail to head end and remove the dark intestinal vein.

PAELLA

Paella, a traditional Spanish dish, is a typical example of the good balance of food found in the Mediterranean diet. A colourful all-in-one dish, it is excellent for an informal dinner party: easy to serve; a good combination of taste and texture; and nutritious, providing carbohydrate, protein and fibre.

SERVES 6

2 skinless chicken breast
  fillets
15-30 ml (1-2 tbsp) olive oil
225 g (8 oz) cleaned squid
125 g (4 oz) scallops
225 g (8 oz) mussels in shells
1 large onion
225 g (8 oz) plum tomatoes
3 garlic cloves, crushed
5 ml (1 tsp) paprika
salt and pepper
600 ml (1 pint) chicken
  stock
15 ml (1 tbsp) tomato purée
350 g (12 oz) risotto rice
  (eg Arborio)
150 ml (¼ pint) dry white
  wine
pinch of saffron threads
2 red peppers
125 g (4 oz) shelled peas
30 ml (2 tbsp) chopped fresh
  parsley

PREPARATION TIME
30 minutes
COOKING TIME
40 minutes
FREEZING
Not suitable

405 CALS PER SERVING

1. Cut each chicken breast crosswise into 4 pieces. Heat 15 ml (1 tbsp) of the oil in a paella pan, large non-stick frying pan or flameproof casserole. Toss the chicken pieces quickly in the oil to brown. Set aside.

2. Pull the ink sac from the squid and discard. Cut off the tentacles and slice the squid into thin rings. Slice each scallop into 2 or 3 rounds, depending on their thickness. Set both aside.

3. Wash the mussels thoroughly in plenty of cold water, scrubbing well, and remove the beards. Discard any which do not close when tapped firmly. Place in a large pan with about 90 ml (6 tbsp) water. Bring to the boil, then cover tightly and cook for 3-4 minutes until the shells have opened; discard any that do not open. Set aside.

4. Peel and finely chop the onion. Immerse the tomatoes in a bowl of boiling water for 1 minute. Remove from the water and pull away the skins. Chop the flesh into 1 cm (½ inch) pieces.

5. Heat the remaining oil in the same pan. Add the onion, tomatoes, garlic, paprika, salt and pepper. Stir well and cook gently for 7-10 minutes, until softened.

6. In another pan, heat the chicken stock to just below boiling point, then stir in the tomato purée.

7. Add the rice to the tomato mixture and cook, stirring, for 1 minute. Pour in 300 ml (½ pint) of the hot stock and the wine. Cook, stirring, for about 7 minutes, until the liquid has been absorbed.

8. Meanwhile, soak the saffron threads in the remaining stock. Add to the rice with the squid, scallops and chicken. Cover and simmer gently for 15 minutes.

9. Meanwhile, preheat the grill and grill the red peppers, turning, until blackened. Cover with a damp tea-towel, leave until cool enough to handle, then remove the skins. Cut the peppers in half, remove the core and seeds, then cut into thin strips.

10. Stir the peppers into the paella with the mussels, peas and parsley. Cook for a further 5 minutes. Check the seasoning and serve immediately, with a salad.

TECHNIQUE

Cut off the tentacles and slice the squid into thin rings.

PAN-FRIED HERRING ROES WITH POTATO PANCAKES

For this quick supper dish all the components can be cooked in the same pan, one after another. Firstly, the pancakes are fried until crisp and golden, then apple slices are sautéed until soft and melting, and finally the herring roes are cooked in butter and lightly seasoned with cayenne pepper. The combination of tastes and textures is quite delicious!

SERVES 4

POTATO PANCAKES
450 g (1 lb) potatoes
½ onion
2 eggs, beaten
30 ml (2 tbsp) plain flour
5 ml (1 tsp) salt
pepper
oil for frying
PAN-FRY
2 eating apples (preferably red-skinned)
75 g (3 oz) butter
575 g (1¼ lb) fresh herring roes
1.25 ml (¼ tsp) cayenne pepper
30 ml (2 tbsp) chopped fresh parsley

PREPARATION TIME
10 minutes
COOKING TIME
20 minutes
FREEZING
Not suitable

525 CALS PER SERVING

1. To make the potato pancakes, grate the potatoes fairly coarsely, then squeeze out as much moisture as possible (see technique).

2. Peel and finely chop the onion. Place the grated potatoes in a bowl and add the onion, eggs, flour and salt. Season with pepper and mix well.

3. Heat enough oil in a frying pan (preferably a non-stick one) to cover the base with a thin layer. Put large spoonfuls of the potato mixture into the pan, flattening them down as you do so; they should be roughly 7.5 cm (3 inches) in diameter. Fry for about 3 minutes on each side until golden and crisp. Repeat to make 8 pancakes in total. Remove from the pan and drain on kitchen paper; keep hot.

4. Wipe the frying pan out with kitchen paper. Core the apples and cut into thickish slices. Melt 25 g (1 oz) butter in the pan and when foaming, add the apple slices. Sauté until softened, but still retaining their shape. Remove from the pan and keep warm.

5. Melt the remaining butter in the pan. When it is beginning to turn brown, add the herring roes and sauté for about

5 minutes until lightly golden. Sprinkle with the cayenne and a little salt and pepper.

6. Put two potato pancakes on each warmed serving plate and divide the fried herring roes between the plates. Spoon the pan juices over the roes. Garnish with the apple slices and a sprinkling of chopped parsley.

VARIATION

Cod's roe can be used in place of the herring roe. However, it must be gently poached first, left to cool, then sliced and fried as directed.

TECHNIQUE

To extract as much moisture as possible from the grated potatoes, place them on a clean piece of muslin, bring the corners together and squeeze tightly.

MEAT

GRILLED STEAKS WITH SHALLOTS AND WINE

An old-fashioned French classic for hurried cooks in search of a treat. Croûtes of French bread are used to mop up the delicious juices from the grill pan and served on the side. A green salad and a bottle of good red wine from Bordeaux are the only other accompaniments you'll need.

SERVES 4

225 g (8 oz) shallots
50 g (2 oz) chilled butter
350 ml (12 fl oz) red
   Bordeaux wine
4 sirloin steaks, each about
   175-200 g (6-7 oz)
30 ml (2 tbsp) vegetable oil
8 slices French bread
10-15 ml (2-3 tsp) Dijon
   mustard
30 ml (2 tbsp) chopped fresh
   parsley
parsley sprigs, to garnish

PREPARATION TIME
15 minutes while grill preheats
COOKING TIME
4-12 minutes
FREEZING
Not suitable

555 CALS PER SERVING

1. Preheat the grill. Peel and chop the shallots. Melt 15 g (½ oz) of the butter in a saucepan. Add the shallots and sauté for a few minutes until slightly softened. Add the wine and bring to the boil. Simmer, uncovered, until the wine is reduced by half and the shallots are soft.

2. Smear the steaks on both sides with the oil and arrange on the grill rack. Cook, as close to the heat as possible, turning the steaks every 2 minutes. Allow 4 minutes (one turn) for very rare steaks; 8 minutes (three turns) for medium. For well-done steaks allow 12 minutes, increasing the time between turns to 3 minutes. Season the steaks with salt and pepper as you make the final turn.

3. Meanwhile, cut the remaining butter into 6 cubes and beat one at a time into the shallot sauce, making sure each one is totally absorbed before adding the next.

4. Transfer the steaks to warmed serving plates and keep warm. Press the bread slices onto the grill pan to soak up the juices, then spread each lightly with Dijon mustard. Put 2 slices beside each steak. Pour the sauce over the steaks, sprinkle with chopped parsley and serve garnished with sprigs of parsley.

NOTE: The technique of beating cold diced butter into a hot wine-based sauce is called 'mounting'. It thickens the sauce slightly and gives a glossy finish.

VARIATIONS

Use rump rather than sirloin steaks. Use a hot griddle pan to cook the steaks, rather than grill them.

TECHNIQUE

After cooking the steaks, rub the slices of French bread around the grill pan to gather up the pan juices.

ORIENTAL BEEF STIR-FRY

Stir-frying is a favourite Chinese cooking method. Here tender strips of beef are stir-fried in an oriental sauce of black and yellow bean sauce, which combines well with the rich earthy flavour of beef. Using lots of vegetables in your cooking increases the amount of fibre, vitamins and minerals in your diet.

SERVES 4-6

350 g (12 oz) fillet steak

2 bunches of spring onions

2 orange peppers

1 red chilli

225 g (8 oz) broccoli

175 g (6 oz) spinach (or pak choi or choi sam)

15 ml (1 tbsp) chilli or stir-fry oil

MARINADE

30 ml (2 tbsp) sherry vinegar

30 ml (2 tbsp) black bean sauce

30 ml (2 tbsp) yellow bean sauce

2.5 cm (1 inch) piece fresh root ginger

15 ml (1 tbsp) dark soy sauce

PREPARATION TIME
20 minutes, plus marinating beef
COOKING TIME
10-15 minutes
FREEZING
Not suitable

200-135 CALS PER SERVING

1. First, prepare the marinade. Mix the sherry vinegar with the black and yellow bean sauces. Peel and crush the ginger and add to the mixture with the soy sauce.

2. Slice the fillet steak into thin strips, about 5 cm (2 inches) long and 1 cm ($\frac{1}{2}$ inch) wide. Stir into the marinade. Cover and leave to marinate in a cool place for at least 30 minutes or up to 12 hours in the refrigerator.

3. Trim the spring onions and cut into diagonal strips about 5 cm (2 inches) long. Cut the peppers and chilli in half, remove and discard the seeds. Slice the peppers into thin strips; cut the chilli into very fine strips. Cut the broccoli into small even florets. Shred the spinach.

4. Drain the meat from the marinade, using a draining spoon. Heat the oil in a large non-stick frying pan or wok, add the meat and cook for 3-4 minutes, stirring. Stir in the vegetables and cook for 3-4 minutes. Stir in the marinade and heat through for 3-4 minutes. Serve immediately, with noodles.

NOTE: Stir-fried food is cooked in minutes in very little oil, so the natural flavours and textures are retained. Swirling the hot oil over the surface of the pan just before adding the food produces an even heat.

TECHNIQUE

Marinate the strips of fillet steak in the sherry vinegar, bean sauce, ginger and soy sauce mixture before stir-frying.

BRAISED HAM WITH MADEIRA MUSTARD SAUCE

This beautiful ham braised in Madeira is served with a piquant creamy mustard sauce, made with the cooking juices. It is large enough to serve 6-8 as a hot main course and leave sufficient to serve cold over the festive holiday. If preferred, you could of course buy a smaller joint.

SERVES 12-16

3.7 kg (6 lb) piece of gammon
½ bottle medium white wine
6 cloves
8 peppercorns
½ bottle Madeira
SAUCE
8 shallots
300 ml (½ pint) dry white
  wine
about 300 ml (½ pint) light
  stock
75 g (3 oz) butter
40 g (1½ oz) plain flour
6 juniper berries, crushed
6 dried green peppercorns,
  crushed
120 ml (4 fl oz) white wine
  vinegar
30 ml (2 tbsp) Dijon
  mustard
120 ml (4 fl oz) crème
  fraîche or soured cream
salt and pepper

PREPARATION TIME
30 minutes, plus overnight
soaking
COOKING TIME
About 3¼-3½ hours
FREEZING
Suitable: Sauce only

625-515 CALS PER SERVING

1. Cover the gammon with cold water and leave to soak overnight. Scrub the skin and drain and dry well. Weigh the gammon and calculate the poaching time, allowing 25 minutes per 450 g (1 lb).

2. Place the gammon in a large pan and cover with cold water. Bring slowly to the boil, then drain off the water. Pour the wine into the pan and add the cloves and peppercorns and enough hot water to cover. Cover and simmer very gently for the calculated time. Allow the gammon to cool in the liquid, then drain.

3. Preheat the oven to 180°C (350°F) Mark 4. Strip the rind off the gammon and score the fat into a diamond pattern. Place the gammon in a roasting tin and pour over the Madeira. Braise in the oven for 45 minutes to 1 hour, basting frequently, until golden brown.

4. Meanwhile, peel and chop the shallots. Transfer the gammon to a platter, cover loosely and keep warm while making the sauce.

5. Pour off the juices from the roasting tin into a measuring jug and wait for the fat to rise to the surface. Skim off the fat and reserve 30 ml (2 tbsp). Make the braising liquid up to 1.2 litres (2 pints) with the wine and stock.

6. Melt the butter and reserved ham fat in a saucepan. Add the flour and cook, stirring, for 3-4 minutes until foaming. Whisk in the wine and stock mixture. Add the juniper berries and half the shallots. Bring to the boil and simmer for 10 minutes.

7. Meanwhile, put the green peppercorns, remaining shallots and vinegar in a saucepan and reduce to 10 ml (2 tsp). Dip the base of the pan into cold water to stop the reduction. Stir the Madeira sauce into the reduced vinegar with the mustard and simmer for at least 15 minutes. Stir in the crème fraîche or cream and bring to the boil. Check the seasoning. Pour into a warmed sauceboat.

8. Slice the ham and serve with the sauce and seasonal vegetables.

TECHNIQUE

Before braising, score the gammon fat in a diamond pattern, using a sharp knife.

BACON, POTATO AND MUSHROOM GRATIN

A satisfyingly self-indulgent supper dish for two, simple to knock together late in the evening when you've been busy with other things. Serve with a crisp leafy salad and a glass of wine.

250 g (9 oz) small new
   potatoes
salt and pepper
1 small onion
125 g (4 oz) bacon, derinded
30 ml (2 tbsp) olive oil
125 g (4 oz) mushrooms
125 g (4 oz) Cheddar cheese

PREPARATION TIME
5 minutes
COOKING TIME
20 minutes
FREEZING
Not suitable

595 CALS PER SERVING

1. Wash the potatoes and halve them (unless they are very small). Cook in salted water until tender. Drain thoroughly.

2. In the meantime, peel and chop the onion; dice the bacon. Heat the olive oil in a frying pan and add the onion and bacon. Cook gently, stirring frequently, to soften the onion and crisp the bacon. Meanwhile, wipe the mushrooms. Leave very small button mushrooms whole; halve or slice larger ones. Add them to the bacon towards the end of cooking and stir-cook for 2-3 minutes. Preheat the grill.

3. Transfer the bacon, onion and mushrooms to a flameproof gratin dish and stir in the potatoes. Season with pepper only, and grate the cheese all over the surface. Grill until the cheese is bubbling, then serve immediately.

NOTE: It's important to cook the diced bacon and onion slowly and to stir frequently.

VARIATION

For a vegetarian version, replace the bacon with sliced leeks, increasing the olive oil by 15 ml (1 tbsp) and adding a sprinkling of thyme.

TECHNIQUE

Add the mushrooms to the fried onion and bacon mixture towards the end of cooking and stir-cook for 2-3 minutes.

GLAZED PORK LOIN WITH FIG STUFFING

A tender loin of pork rolled around a tasty fig, apple and rosemary stuffing, then roasted until the crackling is a deep mahogany brown and deliciously crisp. It is important to score the crackling deeply to ensure a crisp result. The crackling bastes the meat during cooking and keeps it moist.

1.4 kg (3 lb) boned loin of
  pork, skin well scored
salt and pepper
FIG STUFFING
4 shallots
1 garlic clove
225 g (8 oz) no-need-to-soak
  dried figs
1 eating apple
2 fresh rosemary sprigs
50 g (2 oz) butter
finely grated rind and juice
  of 1 lemon
45 ml (3 tbsp) dry sherry
GLAZE
60 ml (4 tbsp) thin honey
10 ml (2 tsp) mustard
  powder
finely grated rind of 1 lemon
TO GARNISH
rosemary sprigs
few fresh figs

PREPARATION TIME
30 minutes
COOKING TIME
2 hours
FREEZING
Not suitable

480 CALS PER SERVING

1. For the stuffing, peel and finely chop the shallots. Crush the garlic. Roughly chop the figs. Peel, core and finely chop the apple. Chop the rosemary.

2. Melt the butter in a saucepan and add the shallots and garlic. Cook for 5-10 minutes until soft and golden. Stir in the figs, apple, rosemary, lemon rind and juice, and sherry. Cook, stirring, for 5 minutes until slightly softened and most of the liquid has evaporated. Cool.

3. Preheat the oven to 190°C (375°F) Mark 5. Lay the pork loin, skin-side down, on a clean surface. Season well with salt and pepper and spread the stuffing along the middle. Roll up and tie at intervals with fine string. Place in a roasting tin and roast in the oven for 1 hour.

4. Meanwhile, make the glaze. Place the honey, mustard and lemon rind in a saucepan and heat gently, stirring. Brush over the pork skin and roast for a further 45 minutes, basting every 15 minutes with the glaze.

5. Leave the meat to rest in a warm place for 15 minutes. Carve into thick slices and serve garnished with sprigs of rosemary. Accompany with a gravy made from the pan juices if wished, and seasonal vegetables.

NOTE: If you buy a pork loin without crackling, brown it all over in butter after stuffing, before roasting.

Any leftover stuffing can be used to fill halved and cored eating apples. Roast around the joint for the last 20 minutes and serve as an accompaniment.

VARIATION

Replace the figs with no-need-to-soak stoned prunes or apricots. Use thyme instead of rosemary.

TECHNIQUE

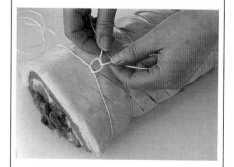

Tie the stuffed pork loin at regular intervals with fine cotton string to secure the stuffing.

SPICED LAMB WITH SPINACH AND POTATO

Lean and tender lamb leg steaks cook quickly under the grill. Here they are finished with a creamy topping that bathes the meat in spices as it melts to a rich golden sauce. Spicy vegetables are the perfect complement.

SERVES 4

4 boneless leg steaks of
   lamb, each about 150-175 g
   (5-6 oz)
juice of 1 lemon
3 garlic cloves, crushed
15 ml (1 tbsp) chilli oil (see
   note)
1 onion
575 g (1¼ lb) small new
   potatoes
10 ml (2 tsp) mustard seeds
60 ml (4 tbsp) vegetable oil
300 g (10 oz) packet frozen
   leaf spinach
salt and pepper
5 ml (1 tsp) ground cumin
5 cm (2 inch) piece fresh
   root ginger
7.5 ml (1½ tsp) turmeric
60 ml (4 tbsp) crème fraîche
   or Greek yogurt
few mint leaves, shredded
cayenne pepper, to taste
mint sprigs, to garnish

PREPARATION TIME
15 minutes
COOKING TIME
25 minutes
FREEZING
Not suitable

545 CALS PER SERVING

1. Lay the lamb steaks in a shallow dish and sprinkle with half of the lemon juice. Spread half of the garlic over the meat, then sprinkle a few drops of chilli oil onto both sides of each steak. Rub the garlic, oil and lemon juice well into the meat.

2. Peel and chop the onion. Wash the potatoes and halve any larger ones. Preheat the grill.

3. Put the mustard seeds in a dry heavy-based pan over a medium heat, cover and shake the pan until the popping dies down. Add 45 ml (3 tbsp) of the oil and the chopped onion. Cook, stirring frequently, over a low heat for 5 minutes. Add the potatoes and remaining garlic. Cook for a further 2 minutes.

4. Add the spinach, remaining lemon juice and 5 ml (1 tsp) each of salt and ground cumin. Stir until the spinach thaws, then cover and leave to cook for 15 minutes.

5. Meanwhile, peel and grate the ginger and mix with the turmeric and remaining 15 ml (1 tbsp) oil. Stir in the crème fraîche or yogurt. Season with salt and pepper.

6. Line the rack of the grill pan with foil, lay the lamb steaks on top and grill for 5 minutes on one side. Turn and spread the cream or yogurt mixture over the uncooked side of the meat and return to the grill for 5 minutes.

7. Uncover the vegetables towards the end of the cooking time if there is too much liquid, to allow the excess to evaporate. Just before serving, add the shredded mint, black pepper, and more salt if necessary.

8. Divide the vegetables between warmed serving plates and place the lamb steaks alongside. Sprinkle a little cayenne over each one. Garnish with extra mint sprigs to serve.

NOTE: If you haven't any chilli-flavoured oil, use ordinary vegetable oil adding a dash of Tabasco.

TECHNIQUE

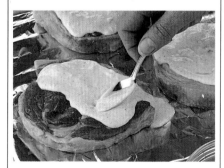

Spread the spiced yogurt over the turned leg steaks.

MINTED LAMB ESCALOPES

Extra-lean, wafer-thin lamb escalopes are flavoured with a fresh-tasting minted yogurt marinade, then grilled to perfection. A colourful salad of baby spinach leaves, tomatoes and onion is the ideal accompaniment. Serve with some warm pitta bread, too.

SERVES 4

450 g (1 lb) lamb escalopes
   (see note)
MARINADE
90 ml (6 tbsp) Greek-style
   yogurt
1 garlic clove, crushed
60 ml (4 tbsp) chopped fresh
   mint
30 ml (2 tbsp) lemon juice
salt and coarsely ground
   black pepper
TO GARNISH
mint sprigs

PREPARATION TIME
10 minutes, plus marinating
COOKING TIME
6 minutes
FREEZING
Not suitable

210 CALS PER SERVING

1. For the marinade, mix the yogurt, crushed garlic, chopped mint and lemon juice together in a shallow non-metallic dish. Season with salt and pepper. Add the lamb escalopes and turn to coat evenly in the yogurt mixture. Cover the dish and leave to marinate in a cool place for 2-3 hours.

2. Preheat the grill to high. Place the lamb escalopes on the grill rack in a single layer. Grill for 3 minutes on each side or until golden brown and cooked through, basting occasionally with the marinade.

3. Transfer the lamb to warmed serving plates and garnish with mint sprigs. Serve with a spinach, tomato and onion salad, and warm pitta bread.

NOTE: For this recipe, you need very thin lean escalopes cut from the leg. These are sold ready-prepared in some supermarkets; alternatively ask your butcher to prepare them for you.

VARIATION

For spiced lamb escalopes, replace the mint with 5 ml (1 tsp) each ground cumin and turmeric, and 2.5 cm (1 inch) piece fresh root ginger, grated.

TECHNIQUE

Add the lamb escalopes to the minted yogurt marinade and turn to coat evenly.

POULTRY AND GAME

CHICKEN WITH CASHEWS

Serve this mildly spiced dish with cinnamon-flavoured basmati rice or a mushroom pilaff. For the latter, simply sauté a little chopped onion, a few sliced mushrooms and a little crushed garlic in butter until softened, then add the rice and boiling stock and simmer until tender. Enrich with a knob of butter just before serving.

SERVES 4-6

about 1.4 kg (3 lb) chicken
    pieces, such as thighs and
    drumsticks
2 large onions
3 garlic cloves
2.5 cm (1 inch) piece fresh
    root ginger
50 g (2 oz) cashew nuts
45 ml (3 tbsp) vegetable oil
1 cinnamon stick
15 ml (1 tbsp) coriander
    seeds
10 ml (2 tsp) cumin seeds
4 cardamom pods
150 ml (¼ pint) thick yogurt
45 ml (3 tbsp) chopped fresh
    coriander (optional)
30 ml (2 tbsp) chopped fresh
    mint (optional)
TO SERVE
yogurt
garam masala
chopped coriander and mint
    (optional)

PREPARATION TIME
15 minutes
COOKING TIME
About 50 minutes
FREEZING
Suitable

400-270 CALS PER SERVING

1. Skin the chicken pieces. If there are any large ones, such as breasts, cut into 2 or 3 pieces.

2. Peel and chop the onions. Peel and crush the garlic. Peel the ginger and chop it finely.

3. Put the cashew nuts in a blender or food processor with 150 ml (¼ pint) water and work until smooth.

4. Heat the oil in a large flameproof casserole and add the onions, garlic, ginger and all the spices. Cook over a high heat for 2-3 minutes, stirring all the time. Add the cashew purée and cook for 1-2 minutes. Add the chicken and stir to coat in the spices.

5. Lower the heat, then add the yogurt a spoonful at a time, followed by another 150 ml (¼ pint) water. Season with salt and pepper. Lower the heat, cover and cook gently for about 45 minutes or until the chicken is cooked right through.

6. Add the coriander and mint if using, and check the seasoning. Serve each portion topped with a spoonful of yogurt and sprinkled with garam masala. Scatter with chopped herbs too, if desired.

VARIATIONS

This works equally well with lean tender lamb or raw prawns. The lamb will take a little longer to cook – simply add more water as necessary to prevent it sticking. If using prawns, simmer the sauce for 15 minutes, add the prawns and cook until they look pink and opaque.

TECHNIQUE

Add the chicken pieces to the casserole and turn to coat in the spices and cashew purée.

LEMON CHICKEN

Corn-fed chicken pieces are marinated in lemon juice, chilli and garlic, with a touch of honey – to help brown the chicken skin during cooking. Ripe, juicy lemon halves are tucked in and around the joints to impart extra flavour during roasting.

1.6 kg (3½ lb) corn-fed or
   free-range chicken, or
   4 chicken joints
4 really ripe juicy lemons
8 garlic cloves
1-2 small red chillies
15 ml (1 tbsp) honey
60 ml (4 tbsp) chopped fresh
   parsley
salt and pepper

PREPARATION TIME
20 minutes, plus marinating
COOKING TIME
45 minutes
FREEZING
Suitable

190 CALS PER SERVING

1. Using a sharp knife and/or poultry shears, cut the whole chicken, if using, into 8 small or 4 large joints. Place the chicken joints, skin-side down, in a large shallow ovenproof baking dish.

2. Halve the lemons, squeeze the juice and pour into a small bowl; reserve the empty lemon halves.

3. Peel and crush two of the garlic cloves and add to the lemon juice. Halve the chilli(es) lengthwise and remove the seeds. Add to the lemon juice with the honey. Stir well, pour over the chicken and tuck the lemon halves around. Cover and leave to marinate for at least 2 hours, turning once or twice.

4. Preheat the oven to 200°C (400°F) Mark 6. Turn the chicken skin-side up. Halve the rest of the garlic cloves and scatter over the chicken. Roast in the oven for 45 minutes or until golden brown and tender. Stir in the parsley and season with salt and pepper to taste. Serve hot, garnished with the roasted lemon halves.

NOTE: This dish relies on the natural sweetness of really ripe lemons. Do not use under-ripe fruit.

VARIATION

- Spatchcocked poussins may be cooked in the same manner.
- Small oranges or tangerines can be used in place of lemons.

TECHNIQUE

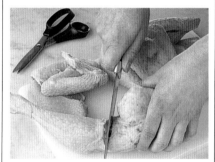

Using a sharp knife and/or poultry shears, cut the whole chicken into 8 small or 4 large joints.

FRENCH ROAST CHICKEN

Roasting the chicken in this way ensures that it is deliciously moist and tender – so it's worth the little extra effort involved. Don't be put off by the amount of garlic – it cooks down to a sweet tasting delicate purée that gives real body to the gravy. This gravy does require giblets which, alas, are missing from most supermarket birds. Instead, search out a good free-range chicken from your butcher or local farm – should you be unsuccessful, make do with chicken or vegetable stock.

SERVES 4

1 roasting chicken, about
   1.4 kg (3 lb), with giblets
1 carrot
1 onion
1 bouquet garni
140 g (4½ oz) butter
2 fresh tarragon sprigs
½ lemon
6 garlic cloves
salt and pepper
10 ml (2 tsp) white flour

PREPARATION TIME
10 minutes
COOKING TIME
About 1¼-1½ hours
FREEZING
Not suitable

470 CALS PER SERVING

1. Preheat the oven to 200°C (400°F) Mark 6. Remove the giblets from the chicken and put them in a saucepan with the carrot, onion, bouquet garni and 600 ml (1 pint) water. Bring to the boil, then cover and simmer for 1 hour while the chicken is cooking.

2. Melt 125 g (4 oz) of the butter. Weigh the chicken and calculate the cooking time, allowing 20 minutes per 450 g (1 lb), plus 20 minutes. Put the tarragon and lemon inside the chicken. Lay the bird on its side in a rack in a roasting tin. Brush the uppermost side with butter. Roast in the oven for 20 minutes of the cooking time.

3. Turn the chicken so that the other side is uppermost, brush with more butter and roast for a further 20 minutes.

4. Turn the chicken again, so that the breast is uppermost. Brush with more butter. Scatter the garlic cloves in the base of the roasting tin. Cook the chicken for the remainder of the cooking time, or until the juices run clear when a thigh is pierced with a skewer.

5. Transfer the chicken to a heated serving dish and leave to rest in a warm place for 10 minutes.

6. To make the gravy, skim off excess fat from the roasting tin. Retrieve the garlic cloves and pop them out of their skins back into the tin; mash with a fork. Strain the giblet stock into the pan and bring to the boil.

7. Beat together the remaining butter and the flour. Whisk this beurre manié, a small piece at a time, into the gravy. Simmer for a few minutes, whisking all the time. Season to taste. Serve the chicken accompanied by the gravy and vegetables of your choice.

VARIATION

Roast whole bulbs of garlic with the chicken, basting occasionally so that they don't burn. Serve as a garnish and encourage guests to scrape out the soft flesh and spread on the chicken.

TECHNIQUE

Pop the tarragon sprigs and lemon half into the cavity of the chicken to impart flavour during roasting.

RICOTTA-FILLED CHICKEN WITH TOMATO AND ORANGE SAUCE

These chicken breasts are filled with a light, fresh mixture of ricotta cheese, herbs and garlic, and served with a delicate sauce of fresh tomatoes simmered with a little orange. Serve them with a mixed leaf salad tossed in a lemon dressing – for a healthy midweek supper.

SERVES 4

175 g (6 oz) ricotta cheese
60 ml (4 tbsp) chopped fresh
　mixed herbs, eg oregano,
　thyme, parsley and chives
2 garlic cloves, crushed
salt and pepper
4 skinless chicken breast
　fillets, each 125-150 g
　(4-5 oz)
4 slices Parma ham
**TOMATO AND ORANGE
　SAUCE**
350 g (12 oz) plum
　tomatoes
2 shallots
1 orange
1 garlic clove, crushed
15 ml (1 tbsp) orange
　marmalade
TO GARNISH
orange wedges
herb sprigs

PREPARATION TIME
20 minutes
COOKING TIME
35-40 minutes
FREEZING Not suitable

315 CALS PER SERVING

1. Preheat the oven to 200°C (400°F) Mark 6. Place the ricotta cheese in a bowl and break up with a wooden spoon. Stir in the chopped herbs, garlic and seasoning.

2. Cut a 5 cm (2 inch) pocket along one side of each chicken breast. Divide the filling into 4 portions and ease a portion into each pocket. Pull the chicken flesh together to encase the filling.

3. Wrap a slice of Parma ham around each chicken breast: lay the ham over the breast, then fold the ends under to enclose and help seal in the filling.

4. Place the chicken breasts in an oven-proof dish, cover with foil and cook in the oven for 35-40 minutes.

5. Meanwhile, make the sauce. Place the tomatoes in a large bowl, pour over enough boiling water to cover and leave for 1 minute. Lift from the bowl and remove the skins. Roughly chop the tomato flesh.

6. Peel and finely chop the shallots. Grate the orange rind, squeeze the juice and pour 30 ml (2 tbsp) into a large pan.

Stir in the chopped tomatoes, garlic and seasoning, cover and place over a medium heat to sweat for a few minutes. Stir in the marmalade. Bring to the boil, then simmer for about 20 minutes, until the mixture is of a spooning consistency.

7. To serve, place the chicken breasts on warmed serving plates, spoon over the sauce and garnish with orange wedges and herbs. Serve with a mixed green salad.

TECHNIQUE

Cut a 5 cm (2 inch) slit along the thicker side of each chicken breast. Open up to form a pocket and fill with the ricotta mixture.

THAI CHICKEN CURRY

Serve this exotic curry with a mountain of boiled rice to mop up the delicious juices, and plenty of stir-fried green vegetables. As a main course on its own, rather than part of a meal composed of lots of dishes, it will probably only serve 4. Although that's more than one chicken breast each, the delicious sauce encourages over-eating and there's nothing worse than having friends for dinner and feeling that you should have made more!

SERVES 4-6

2 garlic cloves

1 medium onion

1 lemon grass stalk

2.5 cm (1 inch) piece fresh
   root ginger

2 small hot chillies

small handful of fresh
   coriander

5 ml (1 tsp) ground
   coriander

grated rind and juice of
   1 lime

2 large tomatoes

6 chicken breast fillets,
   skinned

30 ml (2 tbsp) vegetable oil

30 ml (2 tbsp) nam pla (Thai
   fish sauce)

900 ml (1½ pints) thick
   coconut milk

salt and pepper

TO GARNISH

toasted fresh coconut,
   grated

coriander leaves

red chilli slices (optional)

PREPARATION TIME
15 minutes
COOKING TIME
30 minutes
FREEZING
Suitable

775-520 CALS PER SERVING

1. Peel the garlic cloves. Peel and quarter the onion. Halve the lemon grass. Peel the ginger and cut in half. Put these ingredients in a food processor with the chillies, fresh coriander, ground coriander, lime rind and juice. Process until reduced to a chunky paste, adding a couple of spoonful of water if the mixture gets stuck under the blades.

2. Immerse the tomatoes in a bowl of boiling water for 15-30 seconds, then remove, cool slightly and peel away the skins. Roughly chop the tomato flesh. Cut each chicken breast into 3 pieces.

3. Heat the oil in a large heavy-based frying pan or flameproof casserole. Add the spice paste and cook over a fairly high heat for 3-4 minutes, stirring all the time. Add the chicken and cook for about 5 minutes, stirring to coat in the spice mixture.

4. Add the tomatoes, fish sauce and coconut milk. Bring to the boil, then cover and simmer very gently for about 25 minutes or until the chicken is cooked. Season to taste with salt and pepper. Serve garnished with toasted fresh coconut, coriander leaves, and slices of red chilli if desired.

VARIATION

Replace the chicken with 450 g (1 lb) large raw prawns. Peel and devein, then simmer in the sauce for 5-10 minutes only, until they look pink and opaque. Don't overcook or they will be tough.

TECHNIQUE

Process the garlic, onion, lemon grass, ginger, chillies, fresh and ground coriander, lime rind and juice to a chunky paste.

CHICKEN, POTATO AND SPINACH FRITTATA

For this tempting frittata choose waxy potatoes which hold their shape when sautéed. Look for varieties such as Wilja, Belle de Fonteney and Maris Bard. Some supermarkets print information on bags of potatoes or ask your greengrocer if you need advice. Use a good heavy-based frying pan to cook the frittata, or it will stick.

SERVES 4

450 g (1 lb) waxy potatoes

2 onions

225 g (8 oz) cooked chicken
   or turkey

about 60 ml (4 tbsp) olive oil

1 garlic clove, crushed
   (optional)

handful of baby spinach
   leaves or 1 large
   courgette

salt and pepper

freshly grated nutmeg

5 eggs (size 1)

PREPARATION TIME
10 minutes
COOKING TIME
20 minutes
FREEZING
Not suitable

350 CALS PER SERVING

1. Peel the potatoes and cut into 2.5 cm (1 inch) chunks. Peel the onions, cut in half, then slice. Cut the chicken or turkey into bite-sized pieces.

2. Heat half of the oil in a heavy-based, preferably non-stick, frying pan. Add the potatoes, onions and garlic, if using. Cook over a high heat until the vegetables are tinged with brown. Reduce the heat and continue cooking, stirring occasionally, until the potatoes are cooked. If the mixture starts to stick, add a little more oil.

3. When the potatoes are cooked, add the chicken or turkey and cook over a high heat for 5 minutes or until the chicken is heated through. Meanwhile trim the spinach or slice the courgette. Add to the pan and season with salt, pepper and nutmeg. If using courgette, cook for a further 2 minutes to soften.

4. Add a little extra oil to coat the bottom of the pan if necessary. Heat for 1 minute, then add the beaten eggs. Continue cooking over a high heat for about 2 minutes, to set the egg at the bottom, then lower the heat and cook until the egg at the top is just set.

5. Remove the pan from the heat. Using a palette knife, carefully loosen the frittata around the edge. Invert a plate over the pan, then turn the plate and pan over to release the frittata onto the plate. Slide the frittata back into the pan and cook for 1-2 minutes more. Serve immediately, accompanied by a tomato salad and crusty bread.

VARIATION

Add some chopped salami and a handful of olives at stage 3.

TECHNIQUE

Pour the beaten eggs evenly over the ingredients in the pan.

CHICKEN PANINO

A good medium-sized round loaf with a crisp crust is essential for this recipe. The Italian *paglieno* loaf – available from Italian delicatessens, larger supermarkets and specialist bakers – is ideal, but any similar loaf will do. The quantities for the filling ingredients are deliberately vague, as much will depend on the size of your loaf. Do make sure that you pack the filling in well, so that the whole thing holds together when cut. Serve panino as a summer lunch, or as part of a picnic.

SERVES 8

1 large crusty loaf
FILLING
1 large aubergine
salt and pepper
3 large courgettes
chilli, garlic or virgin olive
    oil, for brushing
6 red or orange peppers
2 beef tomatoes, sliced
about 225 g (8 oz) Parma
    ham or thinly sliced
    smoked ham
about 275 g (10 oz) thinly
    sliced cooked chicken
marinated artichokes
    (optional), sliced
few sun-dried tomatoes
    (optional)
few stoned olives (optional)
generous handful of rocket
    or large basil leaves

PREPARATION TIME
40 minutes, plus overnight
chilling
COOKING TIME
10 minutes
FREEZING
Not suitable

300 CALS PER SERVING

1. To prepare the filling, slice the aubergine, sprinkle generously with salt and layer in a colander. Leave for 30 minutes – the salt will draw out the bitter juices and excess water.

2. Meanwhile, thinly slice the courgettes, brush with a little oil and cook under a hot grill for a couple of minutes each side until just tinged with brown and softened but still retaining some bite. Season with salt and pepper and leave to cool.

3. Drain the aubergine slices and rinse thoroughly in cold running water. Pat dry, then brush with a little oil and cook under a hot grill for a few minutes each side until tender. Season with salt and pepper and leave to cool.

4. Cut the peppers in half. Remove the cores and seeds. Arrange cut-side down in a grill pan and cook until the skins are blackened and charred. Cover with a cloth and leave until cool enough to handle, then peel off the skins. Leave to cool completely.

5. Cut a large slice from the rounded top of the bread and set aside. Carefully remove the soft bread from inside the loaf, leaving a 2.5-4 cm (1-1½ inch) shell within the crust. Brush the inside of the loaf with oil.

6. Layer all the filling ingredients into the bread shell, seasoning well and drizzling with a little oil between each layer. Try to arrange the ingredients so as to give a good contrast of colours between the layers.

7. Replace the bread lid. Wrap the whole loaf in foil. Put it in the refrigerator with a weight on top and leave overnight.

8. The next day, unwrap the loaf and cut into wedges, using a serrated knife, to serve.

NOTE: To make your own garlic or chilli oil simply immerse blanched, skinned garlic cloves or whole chillies in good quality oil for at least 2 weeks.

TECHNIQUE

Carefully scoop out the soft bread from inside the loaf, leaving a 2.5-4 cm (1-1½ inch) shell.

DUCK BREASTS WITH RÖSTI AND APPLE

Rosy pink, tender slices of 'roasted' duck breast are served on golden apple and potato cakes and accompanied by sautéed caramelised apple slices. The method used to cook the duck breasts encourages most of the fat to run out and the skin becomes deliciously crisp and brown. If possible buy the large French *magrets* – one of these easily serves two. Otherwise you will need four standard sized duck breasts.

SERVES 4

2 large duck breast fillets,
    each about 350 g (12 oz),
    or 4 medium duck breast
    fillets (at room
    temperature)
salt and pepper
15 ml (1 tbsp) red wine
    vinegar
60 ml (4 tbsp) apple juice
RÖSTI
2 large old potatoes, about
    450 g (1 lb) total weight
1 dessert apple
2 fresh sage leaves
oil, for frying
TO GARNISH
sautéed apple slices
sage sprigs

PREPARATION TIME
30 minutes
COOKING TIME
20-25 minutes
FREEZING
Not suitable

430 CALS PER SERVING

1. Use a sharp knife to score through the skin side of the duck. Rub with salt and pepper. Leave at room temperature for 15 minutes.

2. To make the rösti, peel and finely grate the potatoes and apple. Squeeze out as much moisture as possible and place in a bowl. Chop the sage and mix with the potato and apple. Season well with salt and pepper.

3. Preheat the oven to 150°C (300°F) Mark 2. Heat 15 ml (1 tbsp) oil in a small heavy-based frying pan. Place 2 large tablespoonfuls of the potato mixture in the pan, pressing down hard with a fish slice. Cook for 2 minutes or until golden brown on the underside; turn over and cook until crisp and golden. Remove and drain on kitchen paper. Repeat with the remaining mixture until you have at least 8 rösti. Keep warm in the oven while cooking the duck.

4. Preheat a heavy flameproof casserole. Add the duck breasts skin-side down and cook over a medium heat for 7-10 minutes depending on size, without moving them; the fat that runs out will prevent them sticking. Turn the breasts over and cook for 3-4 minutes, depending on size.

5. Using a slotted spoon, transfer the duck breasts to a warmed serving dish. Cover and leave in the warm oven for 10 minutes to relax and become evenly 'rosy' inside. Meanwhile pour of all the fat from the pan. Add the wine vinegar and apple juice. Bring to the boil and reduce slightly.

6. To serve, place two rösti on each warmed serving plate. Slice the duck thickly and arrange evenly on top of the rösti. Spoon on the sauce and serve immediately, garnished with sautéed apple slices and sage.

TECHNIQUE

Score through the skin of each duck breast on the diagonal, using a sharp knife. This encourages the fat to run out and the skin to crisp on cooking.

FRENCH ROAST PHEASANT WITH GRAPES AND NUTS

Tender moist pheasants are glazed with clementine juice, crushed grapes and Madeira and roasted to perfection. The liquids in the pan stop the pheasant drying out – especially if you baste during cooking. The pan juices are then used to make a rich and luxurious sauce that's Russian in inspiration.

SERVES 6

6 clementines

700 g (1½ lb) white or red grapes

40 fresh walnuts in shell, or 225 g (8 oz) walnut halves

15 ml (1 tbsp) green tea (Gunpowder or Darjeeling)

200 ml (7 fl oz) Madeira or sweet sherry

2 young pheasants, plucked, drawn and trussed with giblets (see note)

softened butter, for basting

salt and pepper

10 ml (2 tsp) balsamic or sherry vinegar

15 ml (1 tbsp) dark soy sauce

TO GARNISH

extra grapes

pheasant feathers, if available

PREPARATION TIME
45 minutes
COOKING TIME
45 minutes
FREEZING
Not suitable

635 CALS PER SERVING

1. Preheat the oven to 200°C (400°F) Mark 6. Grate the rind from 2 clementines and squeeze the juice from all six; place in a bowl. Reserve the ungrated squeezed halves. Whizz the grapes roughly in a food processor and pour into the clementine juice. Shell the fresh walnuts. Pour 300 ml (½ pint) boiling water over the green tea, leave to steep for 5 minutes, then strain and reserve.

2. Pour half the clementine and grape juice into a roasting tin, adding the Madeira and any giblets (except the liver). Place the reserved clementine halves inside the pheasant cavities. Smear the pheasants with butter and season with salt and pepper.

3. Place the birds in the roasting tin on one side, leg uppermost. Roast in the oven for 15 minutes. Turn the birds over on the other side, baste with the pan juices and roast for another 15 minutes. Finally sit the birds upright, baste well and roast for a final 15 minutes or until done. Test by pushing a skewer into the meatiest part of the thigh; the juices should run clear. Transfer the pheasants to a warmed serving platter and keep warm.

4. Pour the reserved clementine and grape juice into the roasting tin. Stir in the tea, balsamic vinegar and soy sauce.

Place over the heat and bring to the boil, scraping up any sediment from the bottom of the pan. Boil for 1-2 minutes, then strain into a saucepan, pressing the juice through the sieve with the back of a wooden spoon. Stir in the walnuts, bring to the boil and reduce to 450 ml (¾ pint). Taste and season well. The sauce should be slightly syrupy; if not, reduce a little more. Spoon the walnuts around the pheasant and pour the sauce into a warmed sauceboat.

5. Dress the pheasant with grapes and cleaned pheasant feathers, if available. Serve with the sauce.

NOTE: If your butcher is preparing the birds, ask him to keep the feathers and giblets. Or use chicken or turkey giblets.

TECHNIQUE

Baste the pheasants with the pan juices as you turn them, to keep them moist.

VEGETARIAN MAIN COURSES

MUSHROOM AND PARMESAN RISOTTO

This is a wonderfully warming meal for a cold night. If possible, use the Italian risotto rice – Arborio – which has the capacity to absorb plenty of liquid during cooking without turning mushy. Make sure you pare the lemon rind in one large piece, so it's easy to remove.

SERVES 4

1 medium onion

1 lemon

175 g (6 oz) flat mushrooms

225 g (8 oz) broccoli florets

175 g (6 oz) French beans

salt and pepper

30 ml (2 tbsp) olive oil

350 g (12 oz) Arborio
  (risotto) or long-grain
  white rice (see note)

pinch of saffron threads
  (optional)

60 ml (4 tbsp) dry white
  wine

750 ml (1¼ pints) vegetable
  stock

TO SERVE

finely pared Parmesan
  cheese

PREPARATION TIME
15 minutes
COOKING TIME
20 minutes
FREEZING
Not suitable

420 CALS PER SERVING

1. Peel and finely chop the onion. Finely pare the rind from the lemon, using a vegetable peeler, then squeeze the juice. Wipe the mushrooms clean with a damp cloth, then slice.

2. Break the broccoli into small florets. Top and tail the French beans and cut in half lengthways. Blanch the broccoli and beans together in boiling salted water for 3-4 minutes. Drain and refresh under cold running water.

3. Heat the oil in a heavy-based saucepan or flameproof casserole, and cook the onion gently for about 2-3 minutes until beginning to soften. Stir in the rice and saffron, if using. Season well and pour in the wine. Add the pared lemon rind, 30 ml (2 tbsp) lemon juice and the stock. Bring to the boil, stirring.

4. Cover and simmer the risotto for 5 minutes. Stir in the mushrooms, broccoli and French beans. Re-cover and simmer for a further 5 minutes, or until the rice is tender and most of the liquid is absorbed.

5. Discard the lemon rind and transfer the risotto to warmed serving plates. Top with slivers of Parmesan cheese and serve at once.

NOTE: If you use Arborio rice you may need to add a little more stock and cook the risotto for 1-2 minutes longer.

VARIATION

Replace the broccoli and French beans with 400 g (14 oz) fine asparagus, trimmed and halved.

TECHNIQUE

After 5 minutes, gently stir in the mushrooms, broccoli and French beans.

VEGETABLE COUSCOUS

For this quick tasty version of the famous Moroccan dish, couscous grains are steamed over a nourishing spicy vegetable stew. Use quick-cook couscous – which needs to be moistened before cooking but doesn't require lengthy soaking. Vary the vegetables as you like.

SERVES 4

225 g (8 oz) quick-cook
  couscous
225 g (8 oz) aubergine
175 g (6 oz) courgettes
175 g (6 oz) carrots, peeled
1 large onion, peeled
15 ml (1 tbsp) oil
2 garlic cloves, crushed
10 ml (2 tsp) ground cumin
2.5 ml (½ tsp) mild chilli
  seasoning
2.5 ml (½ tsp) ground ginger
60 ml (4 tbsp) tomato purée
1 bay leaf
175 g (6 oz) canned chick
  peas drained, or frozen
  broad beans
750 ml (1¼ pints) vegetable
  stock
salt and pepper
TO GARNISH
chopped parsley
paprika (optional)

PREPARATION TIME
15 minutes
COOKING TIME
15 minutes
FREEZING
Not suitable

260 CALS PER SERVING

1. Moisten the couscous according to the packet instructions. Cut the aubergine and courgettes into chunks. Chop the carrots. Finely chop the onion. Heat the oil in a saucepan (over which a steamer, metal sieve or colander will fit). Add the onion, carrots, garlic and spices and cook gently for 1 minute, stirring occasionally.

2. Add the tomato purée, bay leaf, aubergine, courgettes and chick peas or broad beans. Stir in the stock. Cover and bring to the boil, then uncover and boil rapidly for 8 minutes.

3. Meanwhile, fork the couscous to break up any lumps and spread in a steamer, metal sieve or colander lined with a double thickness of muslin.

4. Place the couscous container over the cooking vegetables. Cover and cook for 5 minutes or until the vegetables are tender, the sauce is well reduced and the couscous is piping hot. Check the seasoning.

5. Spoon the couscous onto a warmed serving dish and fork through. Pile the vegetables and juices on top. Garnish with plenty of chopped parsley and sprinkle with paprika to serve if desired.

VARIATION

Replace the tomato purée with 350 g (12 oz) fresh tomatoes, skinned and quartered. Include other vegetables, such as cauliflower florets, sliced leeks and diced red pepper.

TECHNIQUE

Moisten the couscous grains with warm water, according to packet instructions.

ROOT VEGETABLE AND LENTIL CASSEROLE

This spicy combination of mixed root vegetables and assorted lentils makes an ideal winter supper dish. Serve it with plenty of warm crusty bread and a side salad or seasonal green vegetable, such as broccoli or spinach.

SERVES 6

5 ml (1 tsp) cumin seeds

15 ml (1 tbsp) coriander
  seeds

5 ml (1 tsp) mustard seeds

25 g (1 oz) fresh root ginger

3 onions

450 g (1 lb) carrots

350 g (12 oz) leeks

350 g (12 oz) mooli (white
  radish)

450 g (1 lb) button
  mushrooms

45 ml (3 tbsp) olive oil

2 garlic cloves, crushed

1.25 ml (¼ tsp) turmeric

175 g (6 oz) split red lentils

50 g (2 oz) brown or green
  lentils

salt and pepper

30 ml (2 tbsp) chopped
  coriander leaves (optional)

TO GARNISH

parsley sprigs

PREPARATION TIME
20 minutes
COOKING TIME
About 1 hour
FREEZING
Not suitable

260 CALS PER SERVING

1. Preheat the oven to 180°C (350°F) Mark 4. Crush the cumin, coriander and mustard seeds in a mortar with a pestle (or in a strong bowl with the end of a rolling pin). Peel and grate or finely chop the ginger.

2. Peel and slice the onions and carrots. Clean the leeks thoroughly, then cut into slices. Peel and roughly chop the mooli; halve the mushrooms if large.

3. Heat the oil in a large flameproof casserole. Add the onions, carrots, leeks and mooli, and fry for 2-3 minutes, stirring constantly. Add the mushrooms, garlic, ginger, turmeric and crushed spices, and fry for a further 2-3 minutes, stirring.

4. Rinse the lentils in a colander under cold running water, then drain. Stir the lentils into the casserole with 750 ml (1¼ pints) boiling water. Season with salt and pepper and return to the boil. Cover and cook in the oven for about 45 minutes or until the vegetables and lentils are tender. Stir in the coriander if using, and adjust the seasoning before serving, garnished with parsley.

VARIATION

Replace the mooli (white radish) with parsnips or young turnips.

TECHNIQUE

Use a pestle and mortar to crush the cumin, coriander and mustard seeds.

MIXED ONION CASSEROLE WITH JUNIPER

This delicious casserole is baked slowly in the oven until the onions are partly caramelised and acquire a sweet, mellow flavour. Serve as a tasty accompaniment to a savoury pie or bake. Alternatively, serve with a jacket potato and green beans as a substantial supper dish in its own right.

SERVES 4

6 medium onions

1 bunch of spring onions

6-8 shallots

5 garlic cloves

8 juniper berries

50 g (2 oz) butter

600 ml (1 pint) vegetable stock (approximately)

coarse sea salt and pepper

6 slices French bread, 1 cm (½ inch) thick

125 g (4 oz) coarsely grated vegetarian mature Cheddar cheese

TO GARNISH

15 ml (1 tbsp) snipped chives

PREPARATION TIME
15 minutes
COOKING TIME
1½ hours
FREEZING
Not suitable

460 CALS PER SERVING

1. Preheat the oven to 180°C (350°F) Mark 4.

2. Peel four of the onions, taking care to trim the minimum from the tops and bases. Cut each one crosswise into quarters, leaving the root end intact to ensure the onions do not fall apart during cooking.

3. Peel, halve and slice the remaining ordinary onions. Trim the spring onions, then slice both the white and green parts. Peel the shallots, leaving them whole. Peel the garlic and slice finely. Crush the juniper berries, using a pestle and mortar.

4. Melt the butter in a saucepan, add the sliced ordinary onions, garlic and juniper berries and fry gently until golden. Add 300 ml (½ pint) of the vegetable stock and bring to the boil. Season with salt and pepper.

5. Stand the quarter-cut onions upright in a 1.2 litre (2 pint) casserole and add the shallots and sliced spring onions. Spoon the sautéed onion and garlic mixture on top. Cook, uncovered, in the oven for 1½ hours. After halfway through cooking check from time to time that the liquid hasn't dried out and top up with more stock as necessary. At the end of the cooking time the liquid should be thick and syrupy.

6. About 15 minutes from the end of the cooking time, butter the slices of French bread and arrange butter-side up on top of the onion mixture. Sprinkle with the grated cheese and return to the oven to crisp and brown. (If by the end of the cooking time the cheese has not browned, flash the dish under a hot grill for 1-2 minutes.) Sprinkle with the snipped chives and serve immediately, directly from the casserole.

NOTE: The temperature isn't crucial for this dish, so if you are cooking a main course at a higher temperature, simply position the casserole lower in the oven. Check that it doesn't dry out and cover with a lid if necessary.

TECHNIQUE

Quarter four of the onions crosswise through the middle, without cutting right through, so they remain intact during cooking.

ASPARAGUS, BROAD BEAN AND PARMESAN FRITTATA

An Italian omelette which is cooked slowly over a low heat, the filling stirred into the eggs or scattered over the top; sometimes it is finished off under the grill. A frittata is served perfectly set, never folded. This recipe will serve 4 as a snack, or 2 persons as a meal.

SERVES 2-4

175 g (6 oz) small new
  potatoes
225 g (8 oz) asparagus
225 g (8 oz) frozen broad
  beans, thawed
6 eggs
salt and pepper
50 g (2 oz) freshly grated
  Parmesan cheese
45 ml (3 tbsp) chopped
  mixed fresh herbs, such as
  parsley, oregano and
  thyme
50 g (2 oz) butter

PREPARATION TIME
35 minutes
COOKING TIME
15-20 minutes
FREEZING
Not suitable

720-360 CALS PER SERVING

1. Cook the potatoes in boiling salted water for 15-20 minutes until tender. Allow to cool, then slice thickly.

2. Meanwhile, trim the asparagus, removing any woody parts of the stems. Steam for 12 minutes until tender, then plunge into cold water to set the colour and cool completely.

3. Slip the broad beans out of their waxy skins. Drain the asparagus, pat dry, then cut into short lengths. Mix with the broad beans.

4. Put the eggs in a bowl with a good pinch of salt, plenty of pepper and half of the Parmesan cheese. Beat thoroughly until evenly blended, then stir in the asparagus, broad beans and chopped herbs.

5. Melt 40 g (1½ oz) butter in a 25 cm (10 inch) non-stick heavy-based frying pan. When foaming, pour in the egg mixture. Turn down the heat to as low as possible. Cook for about 15 minutes, until the frittata is set and the top is still a little runny.

6. Preheat the grill. Scatter the cooked sliced potato over the frittata and sprinkle with the remaining Parmesan cheese. Dot with the rest of the butter.

7. Place under the hot grill to lightly brown the cheese and just set the top; don't allow it to brown too much or it will dry out. Slide the frittata onto a warmed dish and cut into wedges to serve.

VARIATION

Lay 4 slices of prosciutto over the top of the lightly set frittata and grill for 2-3 minutes until crisp.

TECHNIQUE

Once thawed, frozen broad beans can be removed easily from their skins. Pinch one end of the skin to squeeze out the bean.

SUMMER VEGETABLE FLAN

Young, tender baby vegetables are set in a creamy cheese filling well flavoured with herbs, and baked in a crisp walnut pastry crust. You can use any selection of summer vegetables – just be sure to blanch or sauté them first and keep the total amount to about 700 g (1½ lb).

SERVES 6

WALNUT PASTRY
50 g (2 oz) walnut pieces
175 g (6 oz) plain flour
pinch of salt
125 g (4 oz) vegetable
    margarine or butter
FILLING
1 garlic clove
175 g (6 oz) courgettes
25 g (1 oz) vegetable
    margarine or butter
175 g (6 oz) broccoli florets
    or baby carrots
175 g (6 oz) thin asparagus
50 g (2 oz) peas
125 g (4 oz) tomatoes
50 g (2 oz) sun-dried
    tomatoes in oil, drained
125 g (4 oz) full-fat soft
    cheese
150 ml (¼ pint) single cream
2 whole eggs, plus 1 egg yolk
30 ml (2 tbsp) chopped fresh
    mixed herbs
salt and pepper
40 g (1½ oz) vegetarian
    mature Cheddar cheese

PREPARATION TIME
40 minutes
COOKING TIME
About 1 hour
FREEZING
Suitable: Baked pastry case only

520 CALS PER SERVING

1. To prepare the nut pastry, spread the walnut pieces on a baking sheet and grill until golden, turning frequently. Allow to cool, then grind to a powder in a blender or food processor.

2. Sift the flour and salt into a bowl and stir in the ground walnuts. Rub in the margarine or butter until the mixture resembles fine breadcrumbs. Using a round-bladed knife, mix in sufficient water to bind the pastry; you will need about 45 ml (3 tbsp). Wrap the pastry in greaseproof paper or cling film and chill in the refrigerator for 30 minutes.

3. Roll out the pastry on a lightly floured surface and use to line a 3 cm (1¼ inch) deep, 23 cm (9 inch) loose-based, fluted flan tin. Prick the base of the flan with a fork and chill for 30 minutes.

4. Preheat the oven to 200°C (400°F) Mark 6. Line the flan case with grease-proof paper and baking beans and bake blind in the oven for 20 minutes or until set, removing the paper and beans for the last 5 minutes. Lower the oven temperature to 180°C (350°F) Mark 4.

5. Meanwhile, prepare the filling. Peel and thinly slice the garlic. Thinly slice the courgettes. Heat the margarine or butter in a pan and sauté the courgettes with the garlic until golden.

6. Peel the carrots (if using) and trim

the broccoli and asparagus. Blanch the carrots, asparagus and peas in boiling salted water for 1-2 minutes. Drain thoroughly. Cut the fresh and sun-dried tomatoes into quarters.

7. Put the soft cheese in a bowl and gradually beat in the cream. Add the eggs, egg yolk, herbs and seasoning, mixing well.

8. Pile all the vegetables into the flan case and pour the cream mixture around them; the vegetables should protrude above the sauce. Grate the cheese over the top. Bake in the oven for 35-40 minutes or until just set. Allow to stand for about 15 minutes before serving warm.

TECHNIQUE

Line the pastry case with greaseproof paper and baking beans to bake blind.

CHEESE SAUSAGE ON APPLE AND WATERCRESS SALAD

Based on a traditional Welsh recipe, these vegetarian sausages fry to a deep golden crust. They are served on a bed of watercress and apple salad, dressed with a walnut vinaigrette. Serve two each as a supper dish: alternatively a single sausage makes a tasty starter.

SERVES 4

125 g (4 oz) Caerphilly
   cheese
200 g (7 oz) fresh white
   breadcrumbs
2.5 ml (½ tsp) dried thyme
30 ml (2 tbsp) finely
   chopped fresh parsley
2 spring onions
salt and pepper
freshly grated nutmeg
2 eggs
a little milk, if necessary
45 ml (3 tbsp) plain white
   flour
10 ml (2 tsp) powdered
   mustard
oil for shallow-frying
SALAD
30 g (¾ oz) walnut halves
10 ml (2 tsp) sherry vinegar
45 ml (3 tbsp) olive oil
15 ml (1 tbsp) walnut oil
1 small red onion
50 g (2 oz) watercress
2 green eating apples

PREPARATION TIME
15 minutes
COOKING TIME
10 minutes
FREEZING
Suitable: Uncooked mixture only

705 CALS PER SERVING

1. Grate the cheese into a bowl and mix with the breadcrumbs, thyme and parsley. Trim and finely chop the spring onions and add to the mixture. Season with a little salt, and generously with pepper and nutmeg. Mix thoroughly.

2. Separate one egg, dropping the white into a shallow dish. In another bowl, beat the whole egg and egg yolk lightly together, then add to the crumb mixture and mix thoroughly. If necessary, moisten with a little milk; the mixture must be soft enough to gather into balls.

3. Prepare the salad dressing. Chop half the walnuts very finely by hand or in a food processor. Beat in the vinegar, olive and walnut oils, and seasoning.

4. Scoop the sausage mixture into 8 balls and shape each one with your hands into a cylindrical sausage. Beat the reserved egg white lightly until frothy. Mix the flour and mustard powder on a plate.

5. Heat the oil for shallow-frying in a frying pan. Brush the sausages lightly all over with egg white then, using 2 forks, roll them in the flour and mustard. Fry the sausages slowly enough to allow them to cook right through, turning frequently to ensure they brown evenly. Drain on kitchen paper.

6. Meanwhile, peel and thinly slice the onion. Trim the watercress. Quarter, core and slice the apples. Toss these ingredients together and arrange on serving plates. Drizzle with the walnut vinaigrette and sprinkle with the remaining walnuts. Serve the cheese sausages piping hot, with the salad.

NOTE: Soft white breadcrumbs are best made in a food processor from day-old bread. The dressing for the salad can be made entirely in a blender or food processor.

VARIATION

Use another sharp white cheese or a strong Cheddar in place of Caerphilly.

TECHNIQUE

Brush the sausages with egg white, then turn each one in the flour and mustard mixture to coat evenly.

Carrot and Coriander Roulade

This savoury carrot cake makes an interesting and tasty dish. The carrot roulade is rolled around a tasty filling of cream cheese flavoured with garlic, herbs and chopped coriander leaves. Serve it in slices with a mixed leaf and herb salad, and toasted granary or walnut bread.

SERVES 4-6

50 g (2 oz) butter or
   vegetable margarine
450 g (1 lb) carrots, grated
4 eggs (size 2), separated
15 ml (1 tbsp) chopped
   coriander leaves
coarse sea salt and pepper
FILLING
175 g (6 oz) soft cheese
   flavoured with garlic and
   herbs
15 ml (1 tbsp) chopped
   coriander leaves
30-45 ml (2-3 tbsp) crème
   fraîche
TO SERVE
assorted salad leaves
herb sprigs, such as dill and
   chervil or parsley

PREPARATION TIME
30 minutes
COOKING TIME
10-15 minutes
FREEZING
Not suitable

340-230 CALS PER SERVING

1. Preheat the oven to 200°C (400°F) Mark 6. Line a 30 x 20 cm (12 x 8 inch) Swiss roll tin with non-stick baking parchment. Coarsely grate the carrots, using a grating disc in a food processor, or by hand.

2. Melt the butter or margarine in a pan, add the carrots and cook gently, stirring frequently, for 5 minutes or until slightly coloured. Transfer to a bowl, allow to cool slightly, then add the egg yolks and coriander and beat well. Season with salt and pepper.

3. Whisk the egg whites in a bowl until firm peaks form, then stir 30 ml (2 tbsp) into the carrot mixture to lighten it. Carefully fold in the rest of the egg whites.

4. Spread the mixture evenly in the prepared tin and bake in the oven for 10-15 minutes until risen and firm to the touch. Turn out onto a sheet of non-stick baking parchment, cover with a clean, damp cloth and allow to cool.

5. Meanwhile, prepare the filling. Put the soft cheese in a bowl. Using a fork, mix in the chopped coriander and enough crème fraîche to yield a smooth, spreading consistency. Taste and adjust the seasoning if necessary.

6. Remove the cloth from the roulade. Spread evenly with the filling, leaving a 1 cm (½ inch) border all round. Carefully roll up from a short side, using the paper to help.

7. To serve, cut the roulade into slices and arrange on individual plates with the salad leaves and herbs.

VARIATION

Bake the carrot mixture in two 18 cm (7 inch) sandwich tins. Turn out and cool on a wire rack, then sandwich together with the filling.

TECHNIQUE

Lightly fold the whisked egg whites into the roulade mixture, using a large metal spoon.

VEGETABLE ACCOMPANIMENTS AND SALADS

GARLIC POTATOES

Chunky 'chips' of potato are cooked with olive oil, garlic and herbs. Rosemary and thyme impart a wonderful woody aroma to the potatoes as they steam. It is essential to use waxy potatoes for this recipe as floury ones would disintegrate. Use a firm variety, such as Maris Piper, Desirée or Romano.

SERVES 4

575 g (1¼ lb) medium-sized
   waxy potatoes
90 ml (6 tbsp) olive oil
4 unpeeled garlic cloves
few fresh thyme or
   rosemary sprigs
25 g (1 oz) butter
crystal salt, for sprinkling

PREPARATION TIME
15 minutes
COOKING TIME
20 minutes
FREEZING
Not suitable

320 CALS PER SERVING

1. Cut the potatoes lengthwise into quarters, then place in a bowl of cold water. Rinse and pat dry with kitchen paper.

2. Heat the oil in a flameproof casserole or heavy-based pan and, when smoking hot, add the potatoes and garlic. Reduce the heat and fry the potatoes, turning, until browned on all sides. Stir in the herbs, cover tightly and allow the potatoes to cook in their own steam for 15 minutes.

3. Remove the lid and turn the heat up to evaporate any water and crisp the potatoes. Add the butter and toss gently.

4. Scatter with plenty of salt and garnish with thyme or rosemary sprigs to serve.

NOTE: It is important to rinse and dry the potatoes, to help prevent them from sticking during cooking.

VARIATION

Fry 125 g (4 oz) chopped derinded pancetta or unsmoked bacon with the potatoes at stage 2.

TECHNIQUE

Fry the potatoes and whole garlic cloves in the hot oil, turning constantly, until browned on all sides.

SWEDE AND CARROTS WITH MUSTARD SEEDS AND GINGER

Swede has often been a much maligned vegetable, yet it has a distinctive flavour which is enhanced by herbs, spices and aromatic ingredients. Swede and carrots go well together, and the addition of mustard seeds and ginger gives the combination a more exciting aspect!

SERVES 4

450 g (1 lb) swede

450 g (1 lb) carrots

2 pieces preserved stem
   ginger in syrup, drained

25 g (1 oz) butter

5 ml (1 tsp) black mustard
   seeds

coarse sea salt and pepper

TO GARNISH

parsley or chervil sprigs

PREPARATION TIME
20 minutes
COOKING TIME
15 minutes
FREEZING
Not suitable

105 CALS PER SERVING

1. Peel the swede and cut into small dice. Peel the carrots and slice thinly. Cook the vegetables separately in boiling salted water until tender.

2. Meanwhile, finely chop the stem ginger. Melt the butter in a small heavy-based saucepan. Add the mustard seeds and heat gently until the seeds begin to pop. Add the chopped ginger and cook for 1 minute over a low heat.

3. Drain the cooked swede and carrots thoroughly, then mash together. Season liberally with freshly ground black pepper and stir in half of the mustard and ginger mixture.

4. Transfer the mashed swede and carrots to a warmed serving dish and drizzle the remaining mustard and ginger mixture over the top. Garnish with parsley or chervil and serve at once.

NOTE: Use a heavy-duty potato masher or a vegetable mill for mashing. Do not use a food processor as this results in an unpleasant glutinous texture.

VARIATION

Make a mustard and ginger cauliflower cheese by tossing cooked cauliflower florets in half of the mustard mixture. Transfer to a gratin dish and spoon on the cheese sauce. Top with the remaining mustard mixture and grated cheese, then brown under the grill.

TECHNIQUE

Mash the carrots and swede together thoroughly, making sure you do not leave any firm lumps.

SHREDDED BRUSSELS SPROUTS WITH BACON

These buttery shredded sprouts are stir-fried with crispy cubes of bacon. They make an interesting change from traditional boiled or steamed Brussels sprouts and look so attractive. Use lightly smoked bacon, buying it in a piece if possible.

1. Trim the Brussels sprouts and shred them very finely. Remove the rind from the bacon, then cut into small cubes.

2. Heat a wok or frying pan and add the bacon. Cook over a high heat, stirring all the time, until the fat runs and the bacon is browning and crisp. Stir in the butter.

3. Toss in the Brussels sprouts and stir-fry over a high heat for 2-3 minutes until they begin to wilt. Pour in the cream, add the caraway seeds and stir-fry for 1 minute. Season with salt, pepper and nutmeg. Transfer to a warmed serving dish. Serve immediately.

NOTE: Cubed gammon would be good instead of bacon but you will need to fry it in a little butter rather than dry-fry.

VARIATION

Replace the Brussels sprouts with Savoy cabbage, or white cabbage.

TECHNIQUE

Cut the Brussels sprouts into fine shreds, using a sharp knife.

PARSNIPS IN A LIME GLAZE

The sweet nature of parsnips will complement almost any meal. Here the tang of lime is used to enhance their flavour. If possible, use young tender parsnips. The sharp glaze can be used with any sweet root vegetable to excellent effect – try it with sweet potatoes or carrots, for example.

SERVES 4

675 g (1½ lb) parsnips
1 lime
50 g (2 oz) butter
25 g (1 oz) light muscovado
  sugar
coarse sea salt and pepper
TO GARNISH
thyme sprigs

PREPARATION TIME
5 minutes
COOKING TIME
15 minutes
FREEZING
Not suitable

225 CALS PER SERVING

1. Peel the parsnips and trim off the tops and roots. Cut in half lengthways. (If using older, tougher parsnips cut into quarters and remove the woody core.) Add to a pan of boiling salted water and cook for 5 minutes.

2. Meanwhile, using a canelle knife or a vegetable peeler, carefully pare thin slivers of rind from the lime; set aside for the garnish. Halve the lime and squeeze out the juice.

3. Melt the butter in a large saucepan together with the sugar. Add the lime juice and heat gently, stirring, to dissolve the sugar.

4. Drain the parsnips thoroughly in a colander, then add to the lime mixture in the saucepan. Toss in the buttery lime mixture and cook over a moderate heat, shaking the pan frequently, for approximately 10 minutes until golden brown.

5. Transfer to a warmed serving dish and garnish with the slivers of lime zest and thyme sprigs.

VARIATIONS

Replace 1 parsnip with 3 eddoes. Peel and halve the eddoes and cook with the parsnips. Alternatively use carrots or turnips instead of parsnips. A handful of walnuts tossed in towards the end of the cooking time adds a delicious crunch.

TECHNIQUE

Toss the par-boiled parsnips in the buttery lime mixture.

106

SUGAR SNAP PEAS IN A MINTED LEMON DRESSING

Sugar snap peas are available all year round and make an excellent accompaniment. Here they are served in a light crème fraîche dressing, flavoured with fresh mint and lemon. Fresh peas are equally good served this way – it's well worth seeking them out during their short season or, better still, grow some yourself . . . the flavour of homegrown peas is incomparable.

SERVES 4

400-450 g (14 oz-1 lb) sugar
   snap peas
SAUCE
60 ml (4 tbsp) crème fraîche
15 ml (1 tbsp) finely
   shredded or chopped
   fresh mint
finely pared or grated rind
   and juice of ½ lemon
90 ml (3 fl oz) yogurt
coarse sea salt and pepper
TO GARNISH
mint sprigs

PREPARATION TIME
10 minutes
COOKING TIME
5-10 minutes
FREEZING
Not suitable

105 CALS PER SERVING

1. Top and tail the sugar snap peas, then steam or cook them in boiling water until just tender.

2. Meanwhile gently heat the crème fraîche in a small saucepan, then add the finely chopped mint, lemon rind and juice, stirring gently. When the sauce is warmed through, add the yogurt; do not overheat at this stage otherwise the sauce may curdle. Season with salt and pepper to taste.

3. Drain the sugar snap peas and transfer to a warmed serving dish. Pour over the minted lemon sauce. Garnish with mint sprigs and serve at once.

VARIATIONS

Instead of sugar snap peas, use mangetouts or fresh peas. You will need 675 g (1½ lb) fresh peas in pods to give the correct shelled weight. Steam or cook in boiling water for 5-10 minutes until tender; continue as above.

   Young broad beans are also delicious steamed and served with this sauce.

TECHNIQUE

Add the mint, lemon rind and juice to the sauce, stirring over a low heat.

CARROT SALAD

This pretty salad is a good accompaniment to spicy meat and fish dishes. You could replace the orange slices with mango or papaya, or use blood oranges when they are in season. A few black olives scattered on top of the salad just before serving provide a striking contrast to the vivid shades of orange.

SERVES 4-6

450 g (1 lb) carrots
2 small thin-skinned oranges
few fresh chives, snipped
few small fresh mint leaves
DRESSING
1-2 garlic cloves
1 green chilli
1 red chilli
60 ml (4 tbsp) vegetable oil
5 ml (1 tsp) black mustard
   seeds
5 ml (1 tsp) cumin seeds
15 ml (1 tbsp) orange juice
15 ml (1 tbsp) lemon juice
salt and pepper
few drops of orange flower
   water

PREPARATION TIME
20 minutes
COOKING TIME
About 5 minutes
FREEZING
Not suitable

190-125 CALS PER SERVING

1. Grate the carrots, using the coarse side of a grater. (Do not use a food processor as it tends to make them very wet.) Pat dry with kitchen paper.

2. Peel the oranges, removing all the bitter white pith. Do this over a bowl to catch the juice (use for the dressing). Cut the oranges into very thin slices. Arrange the orange slices and carrots on a large serving plate and scatter with the chives and mint leaves.

3. To make the dressing, peel and thinly slice the garlic. Slice the chillies, removing the seeds for a milder flavour.

4. Heat half of the oil in a small pan, add the garlic and cook for 1-2 minutes until just golden brown. Add the mustard and cumin seeds and cook over a high heat for 1 minute, stirring all the time. Remove from the heat and add the remaining oil. Leave to cool.

5. Add the orange and lemon juices to the dressing with the chillies and salt and pepper to taste. Pour the dressing over the salad and turn the carrots and orange slices to ensure that they are evenly coated.

6. Leave the salad to stand at room temperature for at least 30 minutes to allow the flavours to develop. Sprinkle with a few drops of orange flower water just before serving, if liked.

NOTE: If using orange flower water, apply sparingly as the flavour can be overpowering.

VARIATIONS

Soak a handful of sultanas or raisins in a little orange juice until plump. Scatter over the salad before serving. For a more substantial salad, add a handful of cooked chick peas too.

TECHNIQUE

Peel the oranges as you would an apple, making sure you remove all the bitter white pith.

POTATO SALAD WITH CELERY, WALNUTS AND BLUE CHEESE

In this warm, tasty salad, the earthy flavour of potato is perfectly complemented by celery, walnuts and blue cheese. The warmth of the cooked potatoes marries the flavours together and melts the blue cheese slightly. It is important to serve the salad immediately, in a warmed dish.

SERVES 4-6

450 g (1 lb) new potatoes
2 garlic cloves (see note)
coarse sea salt and pepper
60 ml (4 tbsp) walnut oil
125 g (4 oz) walnuts
1 celery heart
125 g (4 oz) vegetarian blue
  Stilton cheese
TO GARNISH
thyme sprigs
celery leaves (optional)

PREPARATION TIME
10 minutes
COOKING TIME
15-20 minutes
FREEZING
Not suitable

560-370 CALS PER SERVING

1. Scrub the potatoes clean; cut any larger ones in half. Cook in boiling salted water for 15-20 minutes depending on size, until tender.

2. Meanwhile, peel the garlic and crush with a little salt, using a pestle and mortar. Add the walnut oil and half of the walnuts and work to a thick sauce. Alternatively put the garlic, salt, oil and half of the walnuts in a food processor or blender and whizz to combine.

3. Roughly chop the remaining walnuts. Crumble the cheese into small pieces. Thinly slice the celery, reserving some leaves for garnish if available.

4. When the potatoes are cooked, drain thoroughly and turn into a warmed serving bowl. Immediately add the dressing, celery, remaining walnuts and crumbled cheese and toss lightly. Garnish with thyme, and celery leaves if available, and serve immediately, while the potatoes are still warm and the cheese is melting slightly.

NOTE: If smoked garlic is available, use it for this salad – it will impart a delicious smoky flavour.

VARIATION

Substitute roasted hazelnuts and hazelnut oil for the walnuts and walnut oil.

TECHNIQUE

Use a pestle and mortar to mix the garlic, salt, walnut oil and half of the walnuts to a thick sauce.

APRICOT AND CASHEW NUT SALAD

This is a quick and easy salad to prepare. Dried apricots are soaked in white wine, then tossed with a selection of bitter leaves, carrot and pepper julienne, and chopped coriander. Roasted salted cashews add a delicious crunch. You can of course use any combination of leaves.

SERVES 4-6

125 g (4 oz) dried apricots
150 ml (¼ pint) dry white
   wine, such as Chardonnay
1 head of chicory
50 g (2 oz) watercress
25 g (1 oz) rocket leaves
handful of young spinach
   leaves
1 small carrot
½ medium green pepper
50-75 g (2-3 oz) roasted
   salted cashew nuts
15 ml (1 tbsp) chopped fresh
   coriander

DRESSING

reserved wine from soaking
   apricots
60 ml (4 tbsp) extra-virgin
   olive oil
30 ml (2 tbsp) orange juice
   (freshly squeezed)
5 ml (1 tsp) clear honey
coarse sea salt and pepper

PREPARATION TIME
10-15 minutes, plus soaking
COOKING TIME
Nil
FREEZING
Not suitable

345-230 CALS PER SERVING

1. Cut the apricots into slices, using a sharp knife or scissors. Place in a bowl and pour over the wine. Leave to soak for 2 hours.

2. Meanwhile prepare the salad. Separate the chicory leaves. Wash all the salad leaves and carefully pat dry with kitchen paper. Peel the carrot and cut into julienne strips. Remove the core and seeds from the green pepper and slice thinly. Pick over the watercress, removing any discoloured leaves or tough stalks. Combine all of the salad leaves and vegetables in a salad bowl.

3. To make the dressing, drain the wine from the apricots into a screw-topped jar. Add the olive oil, orange juice, honey and seasoning. Shake well to combine.

4. Add the apricots, cashew nuts and chopped coriander to the salad and toss lightly. Drizzle over some of the dressing; serve the remainder separately.

VARIATION

Replace the apricots with dried pears, and the cashew nuts with pecans. Add 1.25 ml (¼ tsp) French mustard to the dressing.

TECHNIQUE

Wash the salad leaves in a colander under cold running water.

PASTA
AND NOODLES

PASTA WITH CHORIZO

Chorizo is a spicy Spanish sausage, liberally flavoured and coloured with paprika. It is available both raw by the piece, and cured ready to slice and eat. If you are unable to buy it raw in one piece, use cured chorizo – sold pre-packed ins upermarkets – and cook in the sauce for 5 minutes only. A robust red wine is the ideal accompaniment to this rustic dish.

1 onion
2 garlic cloves
30 ml (2 tbsp) olive oil
30 ml (2 tbsp) tomato purée
30 ml (2 tbsp) mild paprika
1 dried chilli
2 bay leaves
2 fresh thyme sprigs
2 fresh rosemary sprigs
150 ml (¼ pint) dry red
   wine
425 g (15 oz) can chopped
   tomatoes
salt and pepper
450 g (1 lb) raw chorizo
   sausage, in one piece
400-450 g (14 oz-1 lb) fresh
   or dried pasta
chopped parsley, to garnish

PREPARATION TIME
10 minutes
COOKING TIME
About 50 minutes
FREEZING
Suitable

950-630 CALS PER SERVING

1. Peel and finely chop the onion. Crush the garlic. Heat the oil in a heavy-based saucepan, add the onion and garlic and sauté for about 5 minutes or until softened. Add the tomato purée and paprika and cook for 2 minutes, stirring all the time.

2. Crumble in the chilli, then add the bay leaves, thyme and rosemary. Pour in the wine and bring to the oil. Cook for 2 minutes, stirring. Add the tomatoes with their juice and bring to the boil again. Lower the heat and simmer gently for 30 minutes. Season generously with salt and pepper.

3. Cut the chorizo sausage into thick slices and add to the sauce. Cook for 15 minutes.

4. Meanwhile bring a large pan of boiling salted water to the boil. Add the pasta, bring back to the boil and stir once. Cook until *al dente*, tender but firm to the bite. Dried pasta will take about 10-12 minutes; fresh pasta 1-5 minutes.

5. Drain the pasta in a colander, shaking it vigorously to remove all water. Divide between warmed individual serving bowls or turn into a large warmed serving bowl. Spoon the sauce on top of the pasta, sprinkle with plenty of chopped parsley and serve immediately.

TECHNIQUE

Add the pasta to the boiling water and stir once to ensure it doesn't stick together.

SPAGHETTI ALLA CARBONARA

This classic Italian pasta dish – with its rich smoky flavour and light, soft scrambled egg texture – is cooked as it should be, with the heat of the spaghetti setting the eggs to give a creamy sauce. If pecorino cheese is unobtainable, simply double the quantity of Parmesan.

SERVES 4-6

125-150 g (4-5 oz) smoked pancetta, in slices (see note)

1 garlic clove, peeled

30 ml (2 tbsp) extra-virgin olive oil

25 g (1 oz) butter

3 eggs

30 ml (2 tbsp) chopped fresh parsley

30 ml (2 tbsp) dry white wine

40 g (1½ oz) Parmesan cheese, grated

40 g (1½ oz) pecorino cheese, grated

salt and pepper

400 g (14 oz) spaghetti

PREPARATION TIME
About 15 minutes
COOKING TIME
About 7 minutes
FREEZING
Not suitable

675- 450 CALS PER SERVING

1. Remove the rind from the pancetta, then cut into tiny strips. Halve the garlic. Heat the oil and butter in a heavy-based pan. Add the pancetta and garlic and cook over a medium heat for 3-4 minutes until the pancetta begins to crisp. Turn off the heat; discard the garlic.

2. Meanwhile, in a mixing bowl large enough to hold the cooked spaghetti later, beat the eggs with the parsley, wine and half of each of the cheeses. Season with salt and pepper.

3. Cook the spaghetti in a large pan of boiling salted water until 'al dente', or according to packet instructions.

4. When the spaghetti is almost cooked, gently reheat the pancetta in the pan. Drain the spaghetti thoroughly, then immediately add to the egg mixture in the bowl with the pancetta. Toss well to cook the eggs until they are creamy. Add the remaining cheeses, toss lightly and serve at once.

NOTE: Smoked pancetta is obtainable from Italian delicatessens. If it is not available use smoked bacon but you will need to increase the quantity to 175-225 g (6-8 oz) to give sufficient flavour.

VARIATION

Spaghetti with smoked salmon and scrambled eggs is prepared in a similar way. Omit the pancetta and garlic. Instead, add 125 g (4 oz) smoked salmon strips to the egg mixture at stage 2. Heat the butter and oil and add with the pasta at stage 4. Finish as above, adding the remaining cheese and tossing in the same way.

TECHNIQUE

Toss the hot pasta and pancetta with the egg mixture. The heat from the pasta will cook the eggs.

SPAGHETTI WITH MUSSELS

This simple dish, spiced with chilli and garlic, relies heavily on the quality of the tomatoes used. The plump mussels and fragrant basil marry well with the intense flavour of the reduced wine and tomato sauce. There is not a lot of sauce – any more would overpower the mussels.

SERVES 4

900 g (2 lb) fresh mussels in shells
900 g (2 lb) really ripe fresh tomatoes
I onion
4 garlic cloves, peeled
6 basil leaves
150 ml (¼ pint) white wine
2 red chillies
30 ml (2 tbsp) olive oil
salt and pepper
450 g (I lb) dried spaghetti
small basil leaves, to garnish

PREPARATION TIME
20 minutes
COOKING TIME
35 minutes
FREEZING
Not suitable

575 CALS PER SERVING

1. Scrub the mussels thoroughly under cold running water and pull off the hairy 'beard' that protrudes from the shell. Discard any mussels with cracked or broken shells, and those that do not close when sharply tapped with the back of a knife.

2. Put the mussels into a large pan with a cupful of water. Cover with a tight-fitting lid and quickly bring to the boil. Cook for about 5 minutes, shaking the pan occasionally, until the mussels have opened. Transfer them to a bowl with a slotted spoon, discarding any unopened ones; set aside.

3. Strain the cooking juices through a muslin-lined sieve to remove any sand or grit; reserve.

4. Quarter the tomatoes and place them in a shallow saucepan. Peel and chop the onion; crush two of the garlic cloves. Add the onion and crushed garlic to the tomatoes with the basil. Bring to the boil and simmer for about 20 minutes until the tomatoes are beginning to disintegrate.

5. Press the tomato sauce through a nylon sieve or mouli to remove the seeds and skins. Return to the rinsed-out pan and pour in the reserved mussel liquid and wine. Bring to the boil and boil rapidly for 5 minutes or until reduced by about half.

6. Chop the other 2 garlic cloves; halve, deseed and chop the chillies. Heat the oil in another pan, add the garlic and chillies and cook until golden. Stir in the tomato sauce and mussels. Cover and simmer for 2-3 minutes until well heated through. Season with salt and pepper to taste.

7. Bring a large pan of salted water to the boil and add the spaghetti. Cook at a fast boil until *al dente*, tender but firm to the bite. Drain, holding back 30 ml (2 tbsp) cooking liquid – this will help the sauce to cling to the pasta. Stir in the mussel sauce. Pile into a large warmed serving dish and sprinkle with basil leaves. Serve immediately.

NOTE: If you prefer not to have the shells in the dish, remove the cooked mussels from their shells in stage 2, when they are cool enough to handle.

TECHNIQUE

Strain the mussel cooking liquor through a muslin-lined sieve to remove any sand or grit.

SPINACH TAGLIATELLE WITH BLUE CHEESE

This tasty main course can be prepared and cooked in a matter of minutes. If you happen to have a local Italian delicatessen which sells freshly made pasta, do use it for this recipe, otherwise dried pasta is fine. Serve as soon as it is ready, accompanied by a mixed salad.

SERVES 4

4-6 spring onions
400 g (14 oz) fresh or dried
  spinach tagliatelle
150 g (5 oz) ricotta cheese
150 g (5 oz) vegetarian blue
  Stilton cheese
150 g (5 oz) crème fraîche
15 ml (1 tbsp) chopped fresh
  coriander leaves
coarse sea salt and pepper
TO GARNISH
coriander sprigs

PREPARATION TIME
5 minutes
COOKING TIME
2-12 minutes
FREEZING
Not suitable

695 CALS PER SERVING

1. Trim the spring onions and finely chop them.

2. Cook the tagliatelle in a large pan of boiling salted water, until *al dente*, tender but still firm to the bite. The worst thing you can do to pasta is to overcook it, so be careful! Fresh pasta will only take 2-3 minutes to cook; for dried pasta, refer to the packet instructions.

3. While the pasta is cooking, crumble the ricotta and Stilton cheeses together into a bowl. Add the crème fraîche and stir to mix well.

4. Drain the pasta thoroughly in a colander and turn into a heated serving dish. Immediately add the crumbled cheese mixture, spring onions and chopped coriander leaves. Using two forks, lift the tagliatelle to coat with the sauce. Garnish with sprigs of coriander and serve immediately.

VARIATION

Replace the spring onions with 225 g (8 oz) leeks. Clean the leeks thoroughly then slice. Sauté in a little olive oil until softened. Add to the pasta with the crumbled cheese mixture and toss well.

TECHNIQUE

Drain the pasta thoroughly in a colander as soon as it is cooked.

PASTA WITH COURGETTES AND BALSAMIC VINEGAR

Courgettes are cooked until meltingly soft and their sweet flavour is enlivened with the addition of balsamic vinegar. Small to medium courgettes work best in this dish and, for the pasta, choose either large ribbons, such as tagliatelle or pappardelle, or shapes such as tubes or twists.

SERVES 4-6

450 g (1 lb) courgettes
1 small onion
2 garlic cloves
75 ml (5 tbsp) extra-virgin
   olive oil
45 ml (3 tbsp) pine nuts
45 ml (3 tbsp) chopped fresh
   parsley
salt and pepper
400 g (14 oz) tagliatelle,
   pappardelle or pasta
   shapes
15-30 ml (1-2 tbsp) balsamic
   vinegar
90 ml (6 tbsp) freshly grated
   Parmesan or pecorino
   cheese

PREPARATION TIME
10 minutes
COOKING TIME
25 minutes
FREEZING
Not suitable

725-480 CALS PER SERVING

1. Cut the courgettes into thin slices. Peel and finely chop the onion and garlic.

2. Heat 30 ml (2 tbsp) olive oil in a large frying pan. Add the pine nuts and cook, stirring, over a medium high heat for 2-3 minutes until lightly browned. Transfer to a small bowl and set aside.

3. Add the remaining 45 ml (3 tbsp) oil to the pan. Stir in the onion and garlic and cook over a gentle heat for 2 minutes to soften. Add the courgettes and increase the heat. Cook, stirring, for about 4 minutes until just beginning to brown.

4. Add the parsley, seasoning and 30 ml (2 tbsp) water to the pan. Cover, lower the heat and cook gently for 15 minutes, stirring twice.

5. Meanwhile, cook the pasta in a large pan of boiling salted water until 'al dente', or according to packet instructions. (Fresh pasta ribbons will need only 2-3 minutes cooking time.)

6. Uncover the courgettes and cook for a moment or two over a high heat, stirring gently, until any excess liquid has evaporated. Remove from the heat and sprinkle with the balsamic vinegar and pine nuts.

7. Drain the pasta thoroughly and add to the courgettes with two thirds of the grated cheese. Toss to mix. Serve at once, sprinkled with the remaining grated Parmesan or pecorino.

NOTE: Balsamic vinegar can be bought at reasonable prices in many supermarkets. If you are buying it from a specialist shop you may find prices vary, depending on the maturity of the vinegar. The longer the vinegar has been matured the more concentrated the flavour, so – although more expensive – you won't need to use as much.

TECHNIQUE

Cook the courgette slices with the onion and garlic over a high heat, stirring constantly, until they are beginning to brown.

126

FETTUCINE WITH GORGONZOLA AND SPINACH

The rich and creamy flavour of this pasta sauce belies its few simple ingredients. Use small young, tender spinach leaves if possible. Larger spinach leaves can be used, but they will need to have their stalks removed and will require shredding or rough chopping before cooking. Serve this pasta dish accompanied by some flavoured bread and, perhaps, a crisp colourful salad.

SERVES 4-6

350 g (12 oz) young leaf
   spinach
225 g (8 oz) gorgonzola
   cheese
75 ml (3 fl oz) milk
25 g (1 oz) butter
salt and pepper
400 g (14 oz) fettucine,
   tagliatelle or long fusilli
TO SERVE
freshly grated nutmeg

PREPARATION TIME
About 15 minutes
COOKING TIME
10 minutes
FREEZING
Not suitable

630-420 CALS PER SERVING

1. Wash the spinach thoroughly and remove any large stalks. Place in a clean saucepan and cook, stirring, over a medium high heat for 2-3 minutes until wilted. There is no need to add extra water – the small amount clinging to the leaves after washing provides sufficient moisture. Drain well in a colander or sieve, pressing out any excess liquid.

2. Cut the gorgonzola into small pieces. Place in a clean pan with the milk and butter. Heat gently, stirring, until melted to a creamy sauce. Stir in the drained spinach. Season to taste with pepper; salt may not be necessary because the gorgonzola is quite salty.

3. Just before serving, cook the pasta in a large pan of boiling salted water until 'al dente' or according to packet instructions. (Fresh pasta will require only 2-3 minutes cooking time.)

4. Drain the pasta thoroughly and add to the sauce. Toss well to mix. Serve at once, sprinkled with a little freshly grated nutmeg.

VARIATIONS

Add 125 g (4 oz) cooked smoked ham, cut into small dice or fine strips, to the sauce with the wilted spinach.

As an alternative to gorgonzola, make this dish with dolcelatte cheese, which will provide a milder, sweeter flavour.

TECHNIQUE

Drain the cooked spinach thoroughly, pressing it with the back of a wooden spoon to remove as much liquid as possible.

PASTA WITH ROASTED VEGETABLES

Pappardelle is a wide ribbon pasta which always looks attractive served with vegetables. Here it is tossed in a light, fresh-flavoured sauce and topped with roasted Mediterranean vegetables, to make a wonderful wholesome dish with an intense flavour.

SERVES 4

1 fennel bulb

2 yellow peppers

1 red onion

2 garlic cloves, peeled

15 ml (1 tbsp) olive oil

150 ml (¼ pint) low-fat bio yogurt

125 g (4 oz) ricotta or other curd cheese

30 ml (2 tbsp) semi-skimmed milk

30 ml (2 tbsp) chopped fresh basil

30 ml (2 tbsp) chopped fresh parsley

salt and pepper

350 g (12 oz) fresh pappardelle or tagliatelle

30 ml (2 tbsp) freshly grated Parmesan cheese

30 ml (2 tbsp) black olives

30 ml (2 tbsp) capers

TO GARNISH

flat-leaf parsley

PREPARATION TIME
20 minutes
COOKING TIME
20-25 minutes
FREEZING
Not suitable

485 CALS PER SERVING

1. Preheat the oven to 220°C (425°F) Mark 7. Trim the fennel and cut lengthwise into slices, about 2.5 cm (1 inch) thick; reserve a few fronds for garnish. Cut the peppers in half, remove the seeds and core and cut into broad 2.5 cm (1 inch) long strips. Peel and slice the onion. Place the vegetables, including the whole garlic cloves, on a baking sheet. Brush lightly with the oil and bake in the oven for 20-25 minutes, until browning along the edges.

2. Meanwhile, place the yogurt, cheese and milk in a bowl. Add the basil and parsley, season liberally with black pepper and mix to form a pale green sauce. Transfer the sauce to a pan and heat through gently.

3. Cook the pasta in a large pan of boiling salted water for 4-5 minutes, until *al dente* (tender but firm to the bite); drain thoroughly. Add to the sauce with the Parmesan and toss well. Transfer to a warmed serving dish.

4. Remove the vegetables from the oven, mix in the olives and capers and serve on top of the pasta. Garnish with flat-leaf parsley and the reserved fennel fronds. Serve at once.

VARIATION

For a roasted ratatouille sauce, replace the fennel with 1 small aubergine; a few tomatoes and 1-2 courgettes. Roast as above. Omit the capers.

TECHNIQUE

Place the prepared vegetables on a baking sheet and brush lightly with oil before roasting.

VEGETARIAN LASAGNE

This vegetarian lasagne has a rich Mediterranean vegetable filling complemented by a set custard-like topping made from goat's cheese, eggs and cream. Use the mild soft young goat's cheese – Chèvre Frais – which is usually sold in tubs for this. Alternatively you can use cream cheese or curd cheese instead.

SERVES 6

4 red, orange or yellow
   peppers
2 medium aubergines
2 onions, peeled
4 garlic cloves, peeled
75 ml (5 tbsp) extra-virgin
   olive oil
45 ml (3 tbsp) chopped fresh
   oregano
75 ml (5 tbsp) red wine or
   water
90 ml (6 tbsp) sun-dred
   tomato paste
salt and pepper
12 sheets dried lasagne
TOPPING
350 g (12 oz) fresh soft
   goat's cheese
2 eggs
150 ml (¼ pint) single
   cream
45 ml (3 tbsp) dry white
   breadcrumbs
30 ml (2 tbsp) freshly grated
   Parmesan cheese

PREPARATION TIME
About 1 hour
COOKING TIME
40 minutes, to bake
FREEZING
Suitable: Before baking

685 CALS PER SERVING

1. Preheat the grill to hot. Grill the whole peppers, turning from time to time, until the skins are blackened and blistered all over. This will take about 20 minutes. Allow to cool slightly, then over a bowl to catch the juices, remove the skins. Chop the flesh, discarding the seeds, and set aside with the juices.

2. Meanwhile, cut the aubergines into 1 cm (½ inch) dice. Place in a colander, rinse, then sprinkle liberally with salt. Leave for 20 minutes, to extract the bitter juices. Rinse again, then blanch in boiling water for 1 minute; drain well.

3. Chop the onions; thinly slice the garlic. Heat the oil in a large saucepan. Add the onions and cook, stirring frequently, for about 8 minutes until soft and golden. Add the garlic and cook for a further 2 minutes. Add the wine and allow to bubble for 1 minute, then stir in the aubergine, oregano and sun-dried tomato paste. Cover and cook over a medium heat for 15-20 minutes, stirring frequently. Remove from the heat and stir in the grilled peppers and seasoning.

4. Preheat the oven to 190°C (375°F) Mark 5. Cook the lasagne in a large pan of boiling salted water until 'al dente' or according to packet instructions. Drain, then drop into a bowl of cold water with 30 ml (2 tbsp) oil added to prevent the sheets from sticking. Drain again and lay on a clean tea towel.

5. Oil a baking dish, measuring about 25 x 18 x 8 cm (10 x 7 x 3½ inches). Spread one third of the filling in the base and then cover with a layer of pasta, trimming to fit the dish as necessary. Add another third of the filling and cover with pasta as before. Cover with the last of the filling and arrange the remaining pasta sheets over the top.

6. To make the topping, place the goats' cheese in a bowl, add the eggs and beat well. Stir in the cream and seasoning. Pour over the lasagne and spread evenly. Sprinkle with the breadcrumbs and Parmesan, then bake for about 35-40 minutes, until heated through and lightly browned on top.

VARIATION

Replace the goat's cheese topping with 350 g (12 oz) mozzarella, cut into slices.

TECHNIQUE

Layer the filling and pasta sheets in the baking dish, trimming to fit as necessary.

GARLIC AND HONEY PORK WITH VEGETABLE NOODLES

Lean, thin cuts of tender meat, pork tenderloins can be quickly cooked in a hot oven. The savoury liquid that flavours the meat during cooking then dresses the vegetables and noodles that accompany it.

SERVES 4

2 pork tenderloins (fillets),
    each about 250 g (9 oz)
5 cm (2 inch) piece fresh
    root ginger
3 garlic cloves, crushed
30 ml (2 tbsp) thin honey
45 ml (3 tbsp) soy sauce
45 ml (3 tbsp) dry sherry
15 ml (1 tbsp) vegetable oil
10 ml (2 tsp) sesame seeds
VEGETABLE NOODLES
1 large yellow pepper
4 spring onions
2 lemon grass stalks
225 g (8 oz) beansprouts
grated rind and juice of
    ½ lemon
15 ml (1 tbsp) sesame oil
125 g (4 oz) rice noodles
30 ml (2 tbsp) vegetable oil

PREPARATION TIME
20 minutes
COOKING TIME
25 minutes
FREEZING
Not suitable

490 CALS PER SERVING

1. Preheat the oven to 220°C (425°F) Mark 7. Trim any fat and membrane from the pork tenderloins and prick them all over with a fork. Arrange them side by side but not touching in a roasting tin.

2. Peel and grate the ginger. Mix the garlic, ginger, honey, soy sauce, sherry and oil together in a bowl, then pour over the pork tenderloins, turning them to coat all over.

3. Roast in the oven for 25 minutes, turning the pork, basting and sprinkling with the sesame seeds after 15 minutes.

4. Meanwhile, prepare the 'vegetable noodles'. Halve the pepper lengthways. Remove the core and seeds, then shred finely. Trim the spring onions and slice diagonally. Remove the coarse outer leaves from the lemon grass, then shred the stalks very thinly. Rinse and drain the beansprouts in a large colander. Mix the lemon rind and juice with the sesame oil.

5. When the meat is ready, leave to stand in the switched-off oven. Put the noodles in a heatproof bowl, pour on boiling water to cover and stir to separate the noodles.

6. Heat the oil in a wok or sauté pan, add the yellow pepper, spring onions and lemon grass and stir-fry for 1 minute. Drain the noodles through the beansprouts in the colander, shake well and add to the stir-fry.

7. Transfer the pork tenderloins to a carving board. Pour the liquid from the roasting tin over the noodle mixture. Add the lemon and sesame oil mixture and stir-fry briefly. Carve the meat into slices, about 5 mm (¼ inch) thick, and serve with the vegetable noodles.

TECHNIQUE

Cut the yellow pepper into long fine slices. Slice the spring onions on the diagonal.

CRISPY NOODLES WITH VEGETABLES

Crisp deep-fried transparent noodles are tossed with stir-fried vegetables and topped with coriander omelette shreds. If preferred, flavour the omelette with 15 ml (1 tbsp) soy sauce instead of coriander.

125 g (4 oz) thin,
   transparent rice noodles
   or rice sticks
vegetable oil, for deep-frying
2.5 cm (1 inch) piece fresh
   root ginger
175 g (6 oz) shiitake or
   button mushrooms
few Chinese leaves
1 red chilli
15 ml (1 tbsp) peanut or
   vegetable oil
125 g (4 oz) mangetouts
75 g (3 oz) beansprouts
30 ml (2 tbsp) soy sauce
30 ml (2 tbsp) dry sherry
5 ml (1 tsp) sugar
CORIANDER OMELETTE
2 eggs
30 ml (2 tbsp) milk
45 ml (3 tbsp) chopped fresh
   coriander
salt and pepper
a little vegetable oil or
   butter, for frying

PREPARATION TIME
20 minutes
COOKING TIME
About 10 minutes
FREEZING
Not suitable

390 CALS PER SERVING

1. To make the omelette, put the eggs, milk, coriander and seasoning in a jug and whisk together, using a fork.

2. Heat a little oil or butter in an omelette pan or small frying pan. Pour in the egg mixture and cook over a high heat until it begins to set. As it sets around the edge, use a palette knife to pull the set mixture towards the middle, letting the uncooked mixture run underneath. Cook until the egg is set all over.

3. Turn the omelette out onto a sheet of non-stick baking parchment and leave to cool. When cool, roll up and cut into thin slices.

4. Break the noodles into lengths, about 7.5 cm (3 inches) long. Heat the oil in a deep-fat fryer to 175°C (345°F). Test the temperature by dropping in a cube of bread – it should sizzle and become golden brown in 1 minute. Cook the noodles in batches. Deep-fry a small handful at a time for about 30 seconds until they swell and puff up. Remove from the pan with a slotted spoon and drain on crumpled kitchen paper. Don't cook too many at a time as they expand on cooking.

5. Peel and shred the ginger. Thickly slice the mushrooms. Coarsely shred the Chinese leaves. Slice the chilli, removing the seeds if a milder flavour is preferred.

6. Heat the peanut oil in a wok. Add the mushrooms and ginger and stir-fry over a high heat for 2 minutes. Add the chilli, mangetouts, beansprouts and shredded leaves and stir-fry for 1 minute. Add the soy sauce, sherry and sugar and cook for 1 minute to heat through. Add the noodles to the pan and toss to mix, being careful not to crush them. (Don't worry if they won't mix properly.)

7. Turn the vegetables and noodles into a warmed serving bowl and top with the omelette shreds. Serve immediately.

VARIATIONS

Stir-fry 50 g (2 oz) cashew nuts or almonds with the vegetables.

TECHNIQUE

When cold roll up the omelette, like a Swiss roll, and cut into thin slices.

DESSERTS

ALMOND AND AMARETTI CHEESECAKE

A light, creamy cheesecake mixture is encased in a crumbly, crunchy almond case and topped with crushed amaretti biscuits. Make the cheesecake a day before you need it – the texture improves on keeping. Serve a fruity accompaniment – nectarines poached in sweetened red or white wine are perfect.

BASE

75 g (3 oz) butter

125 g (4 oz) digestive biscuits

25 g (1 oz) blanched almonds

FILLING

125 g (4 oz) mascarpone cheese

125 g (4 oz) ricotta cheese

50 g (2 oz) caster sugar

2 eggs, separated

2.5 ml (½ tsp) vanilla essence

15 ml (1 tbsp) cornflour

100 ml (3½ fl oz) crème fraîche

TOPPING

50 g (2 oz) amaretti biscuits

NECTARINE COMPOTE

4 ripe nectarines

150 ml (¼ pint) wine

75 g (3 oz) caster sugar

1 vanilla pod

PREPARATION TIME
35 minutes
COOKING TIME
1½ hours
FREEZING
Not suitable

1. Preheat the oven to 150°C (300°F) Mark 2. Grease and line a 20 cm (8 inch) loose-based or springform cake tin. Melt the butter in a small pan. Meanwhile, whizz the biscuits and almonds in a food processor, or crush the biscuits using a rolling pin and chop the almonds finely, then mix into the butter.

2. Spread the biscuit mixture over the base and about 1 cm (½ inch) up the side of the tin, pressing it firmly with the back of a spoon. Set aside.

3. Place the mascarpone and ricotta cheeses in a large bowl and beat together well. Add the sugar, egg yolks, vanilla essence and cornflour and beat again, then fold in the crème fraîche. Whisk the egg whites until holding soft peaks. Stir one third of the egg whites into the cheesecake mixture, then carefully fold in the rest.

4. Pour the mixture into the prepared tin. Crumble the amaretti biscuit into chunky crumbs and scatter over the top. Bake in the oven, just below the middle, for 1½ hours until just firm to the touch. Turn off the heat and leave the cheesecake to cool in the oven.

5. Meanwhile, make the nectarine compote. Halve the nectarines, remove the

stones, then cut into quarters and place in a saucepan with the wine, sugar, vanilla pod and 150 ml (¼ pint) water. Bring slowly to the boil, then reduce the heat, cover and simmer very gently for about 5 minutes until the nectarines are just tender. Allow to cool, then discard the vanilla pod and chill in the refrigerator for several hours.

6. Serve the cheesecake, cut into wedges, with the compote.

NOTE: If mascarpone and/or ricotta are not available, substitute cream cheese and curd cheese respectively.

TECHNIQUE

Press the biscuit mixture evenly over the base and about 1 cm (½ inch) up the side of the tin, using the back of a spoon.

CHOCOLATE CUPS WITH COFFEE SYLLABUB

Circles of melted milk chocolate, loosely draped and set over moulds, make pretty containers for chocolate mousses, custards and other creamy desserts. Here the filling is a whipped syllabub flavoured with espresso coffee and liqueur. Piped chocolate descorations add a professional finishing touch.

CASES
150 g (5 oz) milk chocolate
15 g ('/2 oz) unsalted butter
SYLLABUB
90 ml (3 fl oz) strong black
   coffee
60 ml (4 tbsp) Tia Maria
300 ml ('/2 pint) double
   cream
15 ml (1 tbsp) icing sugar
grated rind of 1 lemon
TO FINISH
piped chocolate decorations
cocoa powder, for dusting
   (optional)

PREPARATION TIME
25 minutes, plus setting and
piped decorations
COOKING TIME
Nil
FREEZING
Not suitable

430 CALS PER SERVING

1. For the cases, break up the chocolate and place in a heatproof bowl set over a pan of simmering water. Add the butter and leave until melted. Draw six 12 cm (5 inch) circles on greaseproof paper. Cut out each one, 1 cm ('/2 inch) outside the drawn circles.

2. Place 6 narrow tumblers, upturned, on a large baking sheet. Spoon half the melted chocolate mixture onto three of the greaseproof paper circles. Using the back of a teaspoon, swirl the chocolate over the circles, making attractive fluted edges which just meet the 12 cm (5 inch) markings.

3. Lift each chocolate-covered circle over a tumbler so that it falls softly around the side. Repeat with the remaining three circles. Chill for at least 1 hour until set firm, then carefully peel away the greaseproof paper. Chill the cases while making the filling.

4. For the syllabub, mix together the coffee and liqueur. Put the cream, icing sugar and lemon rind in a bowl and beat using an electric whisk, until peaking. Gradually blend in the coffee mixture until softly peaking.

5. Spoon the syllabub into the prepared cases, peaking each serving in the centre.

Decorate with piped chocolate decorations and serve at once, dusted with cocoa powder if preferred.

NOTE: Avoid over-whisking the syllabub otherwise it will gradually lose its smooth texture and eventually curdle.

VARIATION

Scatter soft fruits or broken walnuts around the syllabub to serve.

TECHNIQUE

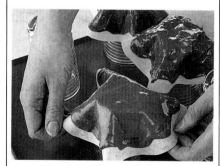

Lift each chocolate-covered greaseproof paper circle over a tumbler so that it flutes softly around the side.

PINEAPPLE AND FIG TART WITH COCONUT PASTRY

This is a fruit tart with the taste of the tropics to conjure up thoughts of warm seas, blue skies and deserted white sandy beaches! A fresh pineapple and fig filling in coconut pastry is hidden by a delicious almond topping. Serve warm, with pouring cream or Greek-style yogurt.

SERVES 6

PASTRY

50 g (2 oz) creamed coconut

175 g (6 oz) plain flour

pinch of salt

100 g (3½ oz) butter or vegetable margarine

25 g (1 oz) icing sugar

a little freshly squeezed lime juice, to bind

FILLING

1 small pineapple

3 figs

TOPPING

125 g (4 oz) butter or vegetable margarine

125 g (4 oz) caster sugar

2 eggs

125 g (4 oz) ground almonds

TO FINISH

icing sugar, for dusting

PREPARATION TIME
30 minutes, plus chilling
COOKING TIME
50-55 minutes
FREEZING
Suitable

730 CALS PER SERVING

1. To make the pastry, dissolve the creamed coconut in 30 ml (2 tbsp) boiling water in a small bowl. Mix to a smooth paste and allow to cool.

2. Sift the flour and salt into a bowl. Cut the butter into pieces and rub into the flour, using your fingertips. Stir in the icing sugar. Using a round-bladed knife, mix in the creamed coconut paste together with the lime juice to form a soft dough. Knead gently in the bowl until smooth. Wrap in cling film and chill in the refrigerator for about 20 minutes.

3. Preheat the oven to 200°C (400°F) Mark 6. Lightly butter a 3 cm (1¼ inch) deep, 23 cm (9 inch) fluted flan tin.

4. Roll out the pastry on a lightly floured surface and use to line the prepared flan tin. Chill again for 20 minutes. Line the pastry case with greaseproof paper or foil and baking beans and bake 'blind' for 10-15 minutes. Remove the paper and beans and return to the oven for 5 minutes to cook the base. Reduce the oven temperature to 180°C (350°F) Mark 4.

5. Meanwhile, cut off the top and bottom of the pineapple and stand it on a board. Cut away the skin, then remove the brown 'eyes' with the tip of a small knife. Quarter the pineapple and cut

away the woody core. Cut the flesh into 2 cm (¾ inch) pieces. Halve the figs and scrape out the flesh into a bowl.

6. To make the topping, cream the butter or margarine and sugar together in a bowl using an electric beater or wooden spoon. Beat in the eggs, then stir in the ground almonds. Spread the fig flesh over the base of the pastry case and arrange the pineapple pieces on top. Spread the almond mixture evenly over the filling. Bake in the centre of the oven for 35-40 minutes or until the topping is set. Check after 30 minutes and, if necessary, cover with foil to prevent over-browning.

7. Serve warm, dusted liberally with icing sugar and accompanied by pouring cream or Greek-style yogurt.

TECHNIQUE

Stand the pineapple on a board, then cut away the skin in vertical strips.

SQUIDGY CINNAMON MERINGUE CAKE

Really a Pavlova in disguise, this meringue – wth its marshmallowy middle – is flavoured with cinnamon and baked in rectangles, then sandwiched together with cream and fromage frais tossed with chunks of fresh strawberries. It is better assemebled an hour or two in advance and allowed to soften slightly. Serve in slices in a pool of cassis-flavoured strawberry sauce.

SERVES 8

MERINGUE
3 egg whites
175 g (6 oz) caster sugar
5 ml (1 tsp) cornflour
2.5 ml ($^{1}/_{2}$ tsp) ground
 cinnamon
5 ml (1 tsp) lemon juice
FILLING
200 ml (7 fl oz) double
 cream
75 g (3 oz) fromage frais
20 ml (4 tsp) vanilla sugar
350 g (12 oz) strawberries
STRAWBERRY SAUCE
450 g (1 lb) strawberries
60 ml (4 tbsp) caster sugar
60 ml (4 tbsp) crème de
 cassis liqueur (optional)
TO FINISH
a little ground cinnamon, for
 dusting

PREPARATION TIME
30 minutes
COOKING TIME
50 minutes
FREEZING
Suitable

300 CALS PER SERVING

1. Preheat the oven to 150°C (300°F) Mark 2. Line two baking sheets with non-stick baking parchment. Draw three 11 x 23 cm (4$^{1}/_{2}$ x 9 inch) rectangles on the paper then turn the paper over to the pencil marks are underneath.

2. Place the egg whites in a large bowl and whisk with an electric beater or large balloon whisk until very stiff. Whisk in the sugar 30 ml (2 tbsp) at a time, whisking well after each addition until the meringue is stiff and shiny. When all the sugar is incorporated, whisk in the cornflour, cinnamon and lemon juice.

3. Pipe or spoon the meringue mixture on to the rectangles on the prepared baking sheets and spread out to fill them evenly. Place in the oven, reduce the temperature to 140°C (275°F) Mark 1 and bake for 50 minutes. Turn off the oven and leave the meringues in the oven until cold.

4. To make the strawberry sauce, either whizz the strawberries in a food processor or blender, then sieve to remove the pips; or simply push them through a sine sieve. Stir in the sugar and liqueur (if using) and chill in the refrigerator until ready to serve.

5. To finish, remove the meringues from the baking sheets, carefully peeling off the paper. For the filling, whip the cream until holding soft peaks and fold into the fromage frais with the vanilla sugar. Chop the strawberries and fold gently into the cream mixture. Sandwich the meringues together with the strawberry mixture, then dust the top with a little cinnamon. Serve, cut into slices, on a pool of the strawberry sauce.

NOTE: If you have a fan-assisted oven, the meringues should bake quite evenly. However in a conventional oven you should switch the baking sheets around halfway through cooking to ensure the meringues cook evenly.

TECHNIQUE

Sandwich the meringue rectangles together with the strawberry cream mixture.

PEACH CROUSTADE

For this hot summer pie, fresh peaches are cooked in a buttery caramel sauce, then encased in delicate filo pastry. The pie is dusted liberally with caster sugar and baked until the crumbled pastry top is dark golden brown, very crisp and caramelised. The recipe is based on a traditional French pie.

SERVES 6

6 large, ripe peaches
100 g (3½ oz) unsalted butter
45 ml (3 tbsp) armagnac (or other brandy)
175 g (6 oz) caster sugar
1 packet filo pastry, about 225 g (8 oz) (see note)

PREPARATION TIME
40 minutes
COOKING TIME
35-40 minutes
FREEZING
Not suitable

385 CALS PER SERVING

1. Immerse the peaches in a large bowl of boiling water for 30 seconds, then lift out with a slotted spoon and slip off the skins. Halve and stone the peaches, then cut into thick slices.

2. Melt half of the butter in a frying pan, add the peach slices and sprinkle with the armagnac and half of the sugar. Cook over a medium heat for 3-5 minutes until just tender, then leave to cool.

3. Preheat the oven to 200°C (400°F) Mark 6. Melt the remaining butter in a small pan and use a little to butter a 23 cm (9 inch) flan tin. Sprinkle 15 ml (1 tbsp) of the remaining sugar over the base of the tin.

4. Lay one sheet of filo pastry in the flan tin, allowing the corners to overlap the edge of the tin. Brush with a little of the butter, then repeat with two more sheets of filo.

5. Spoon the peaches and buttery juices into the flan tin. Flip the corners of the filo into the flan tin, then, one at a time, brush the remaining sheets of filo with butter. Crumple them and arrange on top of the peaches, covering the fruit completely. Tuck in the edges neatly down the side of the tin.

6. Sprinkle the remaining butter and sugar over the top, then bake for 20 minutes. Reduce the oven temperature to 180°C (350°F) Mark 4 and bake for a further 15-20 minutes until the pastry is crisp and golden and the sugar has caramelised. Serve warm with cream.

NOTE: Filo pastry sheets come in a variety of shapes and sizes, but the shape isn't too crucial in this recipe. Make sure though that, when you arrange the first three sheets, the corners are staggered so the tin is lined evenly.

TECHNIQUE

Immersing the peaches in boiling water loosens the skins, so they can then be peeled away quite easily.

MINCEMEAT FLAN

A rich crumbly orange and almond pastry case is filled with homemade mincemeat and banana, then topped with a border of honey-glazed grilled star fruit. The mincemeat needs to be prepared at least 2 weeks ahead to allow time to mature. Alternatively you could buy some 'luxury mincemeat' instead.

MINCEMEAT

1 large cooking apple
50 g (2 oz) glacé cherries
50 g (2 oz) blanched almonds
225 g (8 oz) currants
225 g (8 oz) sultanas
125 g (4 oz) chopped peel
225 g (8 oz) soft dark brown
  sugar
125 g (4 oz) shredded suet
5 ml (1 tsp) ground cinnamon
2.5 ml (½ tsp) grated nutmeg
grated rind and juice of
  1 orange
150 ml (¼ pint) brandy or rum

PASTRY

50 g (2 oz) blanched almonds
125 g (4 oz) plain white flour
grated rind and juice of
  1 orange
50 g (2 oz) caster sugar
50 g (2 oz) butter, cubed
1 egg yolk

TO ASSEMBLE

3 medium bananas
lemon juice, for sprinkling
3 ripe medium star fruit
thin honey, for brushing

PREPARATION TIME
40 minutes, plus standing
COOKING TIME
35-40 minutes
FREEZING
Suitable: Before baking

1. To make the mincemeat, core and grate the apple; roughly chop the cherries and nuts. Place in a large bowl. Work the currants and sultanas in a food processor for 30 seconds, just to break them up, then stir into the apple mixture, together with all the remaining ingredients. Mix well. Cover and leave to macerate for 2 days in a cool place. Pack into sterilised jars and seal.

2. For the pastry, toast the almonds until evenly golden; do not let burn. Allow to cool *completely*, then grind finely in a food processor or electric grinder.

3. Sift the flour and pinch of salt into a bowl and stir in the almonds, orange rind and sugar. Rub in the butter until mixture resembles fine breadcrumbs. Beat the egg yolk with 30 ml (2 tbsp) orange juice and stir into the pastry until it begins to hold together; add more juice if necessary to bind the pastry. Gather the dough into a ball and knead lightly on a clean work surface until smooth. Wrap and chill for at least 1 hour. (The pastry is quite fragile and crumbly).

4. Allow the pastry to come to room temperature. Peel the bananas, cut into cubes and toss in lemon juice. Mix with two thirds of the mincemeat; set aside.

5. Roll out the pastry and use to line a 2.5 cm (1 inch) deep, 23 cm (9 inch) fluted flan tin. Chill for 15 minutes.

6. Preheat the oven to 190°C (375°F) Mark 5. Spoon the mincemeat and banana mixture evenly into the flan. Bake for 35-40 minutes until the pastry is golden brown.

7. Meanwhile, preheat the grill to high. Cut the star fruit into 5 mm (¼ inch) slices and place on a foil-lined grill pan. Brush with a little warmed honey and brown under the grill for 3-5 minutes; watch them closely! Allow to cool.

8. Decorate the flan with the star fruit and serve warm.

NOTE: The basic mincemeat recipe makes about 1.4 kg (3 lb), which is more than you will need for this flan. Use the rest to make individual festive mince pies.

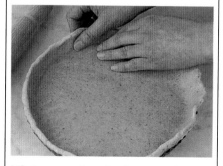

TECHNIQUE

Lift the pastry into the flan tin and press well into the fluted edge. If it breaks, simply patch it up – imperfections won't show!

INDIVIDUAL SUMMER PUDDINGS

An old favourite, individual summer puddings are ideal to serve as part of a healthy diet, especially if you use wholemeal bread. Fruit of any description is good to use as part of a healthy diet – full of vitamins, fruit sugars and fibre, but with very little fat. Summer puddings can be made into autumn puddings by using apples, pears and plums (see variation).

SERVES 6

10-12 large slices of
   wholemeal bread
300 g (10 oz) blackberries
400 g (14 oz) raspberries
125 g (4 oz) gooseberries
175 g (6 oz) redcurrants
150 ml (¼ pint) red grape
   juice
30 ml (2 tbsp) chopped mint
artificial sweetener or sugar,
   to taste
lemon balm or apple mint
   sprigs, to decorate

PREPARATION TIME
30 minutes
COOKING TIME
10-12 minutes
FREEZING
Suitable

160 CALS PER SERVING

1. Line six 150 ml (¼ pint) dariole moulds or individual pudding basins with cling film. Remove the crusts from the bread. Cut a 5 cm (2 inch) circle of bread to fit the base of each mould. Cut six 7.5 cm (3 inch) circles of bread and set aside. Cut the remaining bread into strips and use to line the sides of the moulds completely.

2. Hull the blackberries and raspberries, and top and tail the gooseberries. Strip the redcurrants off their stalks. Place the gooseberries in a saucepan with the grape juice, cover and cook for 5 minutes. Add the remaining fruit and cook gently until the currants start to burst and the juice runs; this will take 5-7 minutes. Stir the mint into the fruit and add artificial sweetener or sugar to taste.

3. While the fruit is still warm, spoon into the lined moulds, using a slotted spoon, and pour on sufficient fruit juice to moisten. Reserve the rest of the fruit juice. Cover with the reserved bread rounds. Top with a saucer or plate and press down with a heavy weight. Place in the refrigerator for several hours or overnight.

4. Turn out the puddings onto serving plates and pour on the reserved juice to cover them. Decorate with lemon balm or apple mint sprigs.

VARIATION

For an autumnal pudding, use cox's apples, pears and plums. Slice the fruit, removing the stones, cores and peel as necessary. Gently poach with apple mint for 10-15 minutes, until tender.

TECHNIQUE

Fill the lined moulds with the warm fruit, using a slotted spoon.

HOT MANGO AND BANANA SALAD

This is a fruit salad with a difference: it's served hot! The delicious combination of tropical tastes, spiked with a little rum, won't ruin your diet – as it provides less than 200 calories per portion. Quick to prepare, it makes an ideal midweek dessert that's something of a treat.

SERVES 4

2 large oranges

2 firm but ripe mangoes, about 700 g (1½ lb) total weight

4 small bananas

25 g (1 oz) very low-fat spread

5 ml (1 tsp) light soft brown sugar

30 ml (2 tbsp) Malibu or rum

30 ml (2 tbsp) lemon or lime juice

PREPARATION TIME
10 minutes
COOKING TIME
5 minutes
FREEZING
Not suitable

200 CALS PER SERVING

1. Thinly pare the rind from one orange and squeeze the juice. Cut the pared rind into very thin strips and blanch in boiling water for 1 minute, to soften. Set the rind and juice aside. Peel the other orange with a serrated knife and slice the flesh crosswise into rounds.

2. Peel the mangoes with a vegetable peeler. Slice the flesh either side of the central stone, then remove any flesh from around the stone. Cut all the flesh into bite-sized pieces. Peel and thickly slice the bananas.

3. Melt the low-fat spread in a large non-stick frying pan. Add the sugar, mango and banana and sauté for 2-3 minutes or until just beginning to soften.

4. Pour in the Malibu or rum, lemon or lime juice and reserved orange juice. Add the orange slices. Bring to the boil, then serve immediately, decorated with the reserved orange rind.

NOTE: Mangoes are ripe when they yield to gentle pressure in your hand.

VARIATION

Guavas and pineapple also combine well with banana and mango and could be used instead of the orange slices, or in addition to make a larger salad. If you like a hint of spice, add 2.5 ml (1 tsp) ground cinnamon.

TECHNIQUE

Slice the mango flesh either side of the central stone.

PEARS WITH A HOT FUDGE SAUCE

A rich, gooey fudge sauce is the perfect foil for delicate slices of juicy dessert pear. For maximum contrast, chill the sliced pears before pouring on the hot sauce. Serve with a spoonful of good quality vanilla ice cream.

SERVES 4

4 large, ripe dessert pears,
  such as Comice or
  William
juice of 1 lemon
SAUCE
75 g (3 oz) butter
15 ml (1 tbsp) golden syrup
75 g (3 oz) soft brown sugar
pinch of salt
60 ml (4 tbsp) evaporated
  milk
TO SERVE
vanilla ice cream

PREPARATION TIME
10 minutes
COOKING TIME
7-8 minutes
FREEZING
Not suitable

325 CALS PER SERVING

1. Peel, halve and core the pears, then cut each half into slices. Arrange on individual serving plates and sprinkle all over with lemon juice to prevent discoloration. Chill in the refrigerator until required.

2. When you are ready to serve the dessert, put the butter, syrup, brown sugar, salt and evaporated milk in a heavy-based pan over a low heat. Stir until the sugar dissolves, then bring to the boil without further stirring.

3. Pour the hot fudge sauce over the chilled pear slices and serve immediately, with ice cream.

NOTE: Allow the sauce to cool a little before serving, especially to children.

VARIATION

The fudge sauce also makes a good topping for plain, nut or praline ice cream.

TECHNIQUE

Stir the ingredients for the hot fudge sauce in a heavy-based pan over a low heat until the sugar dissolves, then bring to the boil without further stirring.

RED FRUIT TERRINE

An unusual way to serve the best of summer's soft fruits. Redcurrants, strawberries and raspberries are layered in a loaf tin to make an attractive fruit terrine. A special dinner party dessert that will be good for your guests – low in fat and high in fibre.

SERVES 6

65 g (2½ oz) caster sugar

275 ml (9 fl oz) medium-dry
   white wine

45 ml (3 tbsp) lemon juice

20 ml (4 tsp) powdered
   gelatine

225 g (8 oz) redcurrants

225 g (8 oz) medium ripe
   strawberries

225 g (8 oz) raspberries

TO DECORATE

mint sprigs

few strawberry slices

small redcurrant sprigs

PREPARATION TIME
55 minutes, plus chilling
COOKING TIME
Nil
FREEZING
Not suitable

100 CALS PER SERVING

1. Put the sugar in a pan with 250 ml (9 fl oz) water. Heat gently until the sugar dissolves, then bring to the boil and simmer for 1 minute. Pour into a bowl, cool, then stir in the wine and lemon juice.

2. Spoon 60 ml (4 tbsp) water into a small bowl and sprinkle over the gelatine. Soak for about 10 minutes or until sponge-like. Stand the bowl over a pan of gently simmering water for 2-3 minutes until it clears and liquefies. Pour into the wine syrup and leave to cool.

3. Strip the redcurrants off their stalks. Hull the strawberries, then slice into 5 mm (¼ inch) thick pieces.

4. Place a 1.1 litre (2 pint) non-stick loaf tin in a roasting pan. Surround the loaf tin with ice cubes and pour in enough cold water to come halfway up the sides of the tin. Arrange a thin layer of redcurrants over the base of the tin and gently spoon over enough liquid jelly to cover. Leave to set.

5. Cover with sliced strawberries, then a layer of raspberries. Repeat the layers, then carefully spoon over the remaining jelly to fill.

6. Leave the mould in the roasting pan until the jelly is just set, then transfer to the refrigerator for at least 3 hours or preferably overnight, to set completely.

7. To serve, fill a large bowl with hot water. Dip the loaf tin in the water for 3-4 seconds, then immediately invert onto a flat platter, gently shaking the tin to release the jelly. Decorate with mint sprigs, strawberry slices and redcurrants. Slice and serve with single cream or yogurt.

TECHNIQUE

Arrange the fruit in layers in the tin, then spoon over the jelly to fill.

FROZEN VANILLA YOGURT WITH STRAWBERRY SAUCE

This is a delicious light frozen yogurt. Made with sheep's milk yogurt which is low in fat, it has a mild tangy flavour that combines well with the strawberry and balsamic vinegar sauce. If you wish to serve this during the winter, accompany with cinnamon-flavoured poached apples instead of strawberry sauce.

SERVES 6

FROZEN YOGURT

150 ml (¼ pint) semi-
  skimmed milk

5 ml (1 tsp) powdered
  gelatine

750 ml (1¼ pints) sheep's
  milk Greek yogurt

125 g (4 oz) Greek or wild
  flower-scented honey

2 egg whites

5 ml (1 tsp) vanilla essence

SAUCE

350 g (12 oz) strawberries

5-10 ml (1-2 tsp) balsamic
  vinegar

TO SERVE

225 g (8 oz) blueberries

lavender flowers, to
  decorate (optional)

PREPARATION TIME
35 minutes
COOKING TIME
Nil
FREEZING Suitable

235 CALS PER SERVING

1. Set the freezer to fast-freeze. Warm the milk in a saucepan until hot but not boiling. Remove from the heat and sprinkle over the gelatine, stirring quickly until it dissolves. Let cool slightly.

2. Mix the yogurt and honey together. When the gelatine has cooled to the same temperature as the yogurt, mix the two together.

3. Whisk the egg whites in a bowl until they form soft peaks, then fold into the yogurt mixture with a metal spoon. Stir in the vanilla essence. Freeze in an ice cream machine, according to manufacturer's instructions. Alternatively, turn into a freezerproof container, cover and freeze for 1½-2 hours, until beginning to freeze around the edge. Remove from the freezer, beat well or work in a food processor for a few seconds. Return to the freezer. Repeat twice more at 30 minute intervals, then freeze until firm.

4. To prepare the sauce, purée the strawberries in a blender or food processor. If preferred, pass the purée through a nylon sieve. Stir the balsamic vinegar into the strawberry purée and pour into a jug.

5. Remove the ice cream from the freezer 20-30 minutes before required, to soften. Scoop into chilled glasses,

pour on the strawberry sauce and top with blueberries. Decorate with lavender flowers if wished.

VARIATION

Fold the strawberry purée into the half-frozen yogurt, after the final beating. Use other puréed fruits to flavour the ice cream. Spoon the half-frozen yogurt into individual ramekin dishes, after the final beating.

TECHNIQUE

Fold the whisked egg whites into the yogurt mixture with a metal spoon.

BAKING

SPICE FINGER BISCUITS

Crisp and light with a slightly chewy centre, these simple finger biscuits have an almost meringue-like texture. The deliciously spicy after-taste is accentuated by the sprinkling of black pepper, although this can be omitted for a more conventional biscuit. Serve with coffee, or as an accompaniment to creamy desserts.

MAKES 16-18

1 egg white
10 ml (2 tsp) cornflour
2.5 ml (½ tsp) ground
cinnamon
2.5 ml (½ tsp) ground ginger
125 g (4 oz) caster sugar
75 g (3 oz) ground almonds
freshly ground black pepper
and extra spice, for
sprinkling

PREPARATION TIME
12 minutes
COOKING TIME
15 minutes
FREEZING
Not suitable

65-50 CALS PER BISCUIT

1. Preheat the oven to 180°C (350°F) Mark 4. Line a large baking sheet with non-stick baking parchment.

2. Whisk the egg white in a bowl until stiff, but not dry. Sift the cornflour and spices over the egg white. Add the sugar and ground almonds and gently stir the ingredients together to form a light sticky paste.

3. Place the mixture in a large piping bag, fitted with a 1 cm (½ inch) plain nozzle. Pipe 7 cm (3 inch) finger lengths onto the baking sheet, spacing them slightly apart. Sprinkle with pepper and a little extra spice and bake for 12 minutes or until crisp and golden. Transfer to a wire rack to cool.

NOTE: If you don't have a suitable piping nozzle, spoon walnut-sized pieces of the mixture onto the lined baking sheet instead.

VARIATIONS

Coriander Biscuits: Substitute ground coriander for the cinnamon and add the grated rind of ½ orange. Sprinkle crushed coriander over the biscuits before baking.

Coconut Biscuits: Replace the spices and ground almonds with 75 g (3 oz) desiccated coconut and add a few drops of almond essence.

TECHNIQUE

Pipe 7.5 cm (3 inch) finger lengths of the mixture onto the lined baking sheet, using a knife to break off the mixture.

LEMON AND CARDAMOM RINGS

Cardamom seeds – crushed to extract their heady fragrance and spicy, lemony flavour – are combined with plenty of lemon zest in these attractive biscuit rings. A deliciously tangy, smooth lemon icing is brushed over the tops of the biscuits after baking.

MAKES ABOUT 14

15 ml (1 tbsp) cardamom
   pods
175 g (6 oz) unsalted butter
50 g (2 oz) caster sugar
225 g (8 oz) plain white flour
finely grated rind of
   2 lemons
20-25 ml (4-5 tsp) lemon
   juice
LEMON ICING
125 g (4 oz) icing sugar
25-35 ml (5-7 tsp) lemon
   juice
TO DECORATE
15 ml (1 tbsp) cardamom
   pods
strips of finely pared lemon
   rind, for sprinkling

PREPARATION TIME
20 minutes, plus chilling
COOKING TIME
10-12 minutes
FREEZING
Not suitable

170 CALS PER BISCUIT

1. Preheat the oven to 180°C (350°F) Mark 4. Lightly grease two baking sheets. Crush the cardamom pods, using a pestle and mortar, to remove the seeds. Discard the pods and lightly crush the seeds.

2. Cream the butter and sugar together in a bowl until pale and fluffy. Beat in the flour, cardamom seeds, lemon rind and enough lemon juice to mix to a smooth paste.

3. Place half of the mixture in a piping bag, fitted with a 1 cm (½ inch) plain nozzle. Pipe a small round of paste onto a baking sheet. Continue piping adjacent small rounds to shape a ring. Repeat with the remaining paste to make about 14 rings. Chill in the refrigerator for about 30 minutes.

4. Bake the biscuits for 10-12 minutes until turning golden around the edges. Transfer to a wire rack to cool.

5. To make the icing, sift the icing sugar into a bowl and mix in enough lemon juice to give the consistency of pouring cream. Brush over the tops of the biscuits. Crush more cardamom seeds, as above, and sprinkle over the biscuits with the lemon rind.

NOTE: Use a lemon zester to pare delicate strips of rind for decoration. Alternatively finely grate the rind.

VARIATIONS

Use grated orange or lime rind and juice in place of the lemon.

TECHNIQUE

Pipe small adjacent rounds of the mixture in circles to form biscuit rings, about 7.5 cm (3 inches) in diameter.

ALMOND FUDGE CRUMBLES

Hidden pieces of crushed almond flakes and chewy fudge marry perfectly in these simple biscuits. Scattered with more crumbled fudge and almonds, they are baked to a cookie-like crumbliness, then served with a dusting of icing sugar. Choose a good quality almond essence to bring out the full almond flavour.

MAKES 24

75 g (3 oz) flaked almonds
50 g (2 oz) vanilla fudge
200 g (7 oz) plain white flour
pinch of salt
2.5 ml (½ tsp) bicarbonate of
  soda
125 g (4 oz) unsalted butter
125 g (4 oz) muscovado
  sugar
1 egg
5 ml (1 tsp) almond essence
TOPPING
25 g (1 oz) flaked almonds
25 g (1 oz) vanilla fudge
icing sugar, for dusting

PREPARATION TIME
10 minutes
COOKING TIME
12 minutes
FREEZING
Suitable

130 CALS PER BISCUIT

1. Preheat the oven to 190°C (375°F) Mark 5. Lightly grease two baking sheets. Crumble the almonds into small flakes. Finely dice the fudge.

2. Sift the flour, salt and bicarbonate of soda into a bowl. Add the butter, cut into small pieces, and rub in using the fingertips. Add the sugar, egg, almond essence, flaked almonds and fudge and mix to a fairly firm dough.

3. Turn onto a lightly floured surface and roll into a cylinder, 23 cm (9 inches) long. Cut the dough into 24 rounds. Place the rounds, slightly apart, on the baking sheets.

4. Lightly crumble the almonds and chop the fudge for the topping. Scatter over the biscuits and press down lightly to adhere. Bake the biscuits for about 12 minutes until turning golden around the edges. Leave on the baking sheets for 5 minutes, then transfer to a wire rack to cool. Serve dusted with icing sugar.

NOTE: Use a slab of vanilla or 'cream' fudge, or individually wrapped sweets.

VARIATIONS

Coffee and Walnut Crumbles: Add 15 ml (1 tbsp) finely ground espresso coffee to the dry ingredients and substitute finely ground walnuts for the almonds.
Apple and Raisin Crumbles: Use raisin fudge and substitute chopped dried apples for half of the almonds.

TECHNIQUE

Cut the cylinder of dough into 24 equal-sized pieces.

CHOCOLATE SOFT CENTRES

These crackled, crumbly biscuits consist of a crisp chocolate 'case' which cleverly conceals a velvet smooth chocolate centre. When served freshly baked the filling literally melts in-the-mouth; if served cool it hardens slightly to an equally delicious fudge-like texture.

MAKES 18

150 g (5 oz) unsalted butter, softened
150 g (5 oz) caster sugar
1 egg yolk
25 g (1 oz) cocoa powder
250 g (9 oz) self-raising flour
18-20 squares plain chocolate, about 125 g (4 oz)

TO FINISH

cocoa powder, for dusting

PREPARATION TIME
20 minutes, plus chilling
COOKING TIME
10 minutes
FREEZING
Suitable

180 CALS PER BISCUIT

1. Lightly grease a large baking sheet. Cream the butter and sugar together in a bowl until pale and fluffy. Beat in the egg yolk. Sift the cocoa powder and flour into the bowl and mix to a firm dough, using a round-bladed knife.

2. Turn out onto a lightly floured surface and knead lightly. Chill in the refrigerator for 30 minutes.

3. Preheat the oven to 190°C (375°F) Mark 5. Roll a third of the dough out thinly on a floured surface and cut out 18 circles, using a 4 cm (1½ inch) cutter. Place on the prepared baking sheet and press a chocolate square into the centre of each one.

4. Roll out the remaining dough and cut out 18 larger circles, using a 5 cm (2 inch) cutter. Lay these over the chocolate bases, securing the edges to enclose the chocolate filling.

5. Bake for 10 minutes or until the biscuits have spread and risen. Leave on the baking sheet for 5 minutes, then transfer to a wire rack to cool. Serve dusted with cocoa powder.

NOTE: The larger circles of dough will crack slightly as you position them over the bases.

VARIATION

Use milk or white chocolate squares to fill the biscuits instead of plain chocolate.

TECHNIQUE

Lay the larger circles of dough over the chocolate bases, moulding and easing them to fit.

WHITE CHOCOLATE BROWNIES

Deliciously moist, laden with chocolate and crusted in a glossy coat of sugar, chocolate brownies are one of the most adorable teatime treats! This white chocolate version, packed with hazelnuts and generous chunks of creamy white chocolate, make an exciting and equally enticing alternative.

MAKES 12

175 g (6 oz) shelled
   hazelnuts
500 g (1 lb 2 oz) white
   chocolate
75 g (3 oz) butter
3 eggs
175 g (6 oz) caster sugar
175 g (6 oz) self-raising
   white flour
pinch of salt
5 ml (1 tsp) vanilla essence

PREPARATION TIME
20 minutes
COOKING TIME
30-35 minutes
FREEZING
Suitable

490 CALS PER BROWNIE

1. Preheat the oven to 190°C (375°F) Mark 5. Grease and line a baking tin measuring 22 × 29 cm (8½ × 11½ inches) across the top and 19 × 27 cm (7½ × 10½ inches) across the base. (Or use a tin with similar dimensions.)

2. Roughly chop the hazelnuts. Roughly chop 400 g (14 oz) of the chocolate and set aside. Break up the remaining chocolate and put into a heatproof bowl with the butter. Place over a pan of simmering water until melted. Leave to cool slightly.

3. Whisk the eggs and sugar together in a large bowl until smooth, then gradually beat in the melted chocolate mixture. Sift the flour and salt over the mixture, then fold in with the hazelnuts, chopped chocolate and vanilla essence.

4. Turn the mixture into the prepared tin and level the surface. Bake for 30-35 minutes until risen and golden, and the centre is just firm to the touch. Leave to cool in the tin. Turn out and cut into 12 squares. Store in an airtight container for up to 1 week.

NOTE: When cooked, the mixture will still be very soft under the crust; it firms up during cooling.

VARIATIONS

Use any other roughly chopped nuts instead of the hazelnuts. Almond, walnuts, pecans and brazil nuts are suitable.

TECHNIQUE

Gradually beat the melted chocolate mixture into the eggs and sugar; the consistency will become quite firm.

DOUBLE CHOCOLATE MUFFINS

Homemade muffins have a deliciously light texture that crumbles into soft, airy pieces of sponge when eaten freshly baked. This dark, chocolately version is richly flavoured with melted chocolate; additional chunks of dark and white chocolate are folded in before baking, too. These give melt-in-the-mouth bites of pure delight!

MAKES 14

300 g (10 oz) plain chocolate
125 g (4 oz) white chocolate
375 g (13 oz) self-raising
   flour
15 ml (1 tbsp) baking
   powder
65 g (2¹/₂ oz) cocoa powder
75 g (3 oz) light muscovado
   sugar
1 egg
1 egg yolk
10 ml (2 tsp) vanilla essence
90 ml (6 tbsp) vegetable oil
375 ml (13 fl oz) milk
icing sugar or cocoa
   powder, for dusting
   (optional)

PREPARATION TIME
15 minutes
COOKING TIME
25 minutes
FREEZING
Suitable

370 CALS PER MUFFING

1. preheat the oven to 220°C (425°F) Mark 7. Line 14 deep bun tins or muffin tins with apper muffin cases. Break up 175 g (6 oz) of the plain chocolate and melt in a heatproof bowl set over a saucepan of simmering water.

2. Roughly chop the remaining plain and white chocolate. Sift the flour, baking powder and cocoa powder into a bowl. Stir in the sugar.

3. In another bowl, beat together the egg, egg yolk, vanilla essence, oil, melted chocolate and milk. Add to the dry ingredients with the chopped chocolate and stir the ingredients together quickly until the flour is only just incorporated; do not over-mix.

4. Spoon the mixture into the paper cases, piling it up in the centre. Bake for 25 minutes until the muffins are well risen and craggy in appearance. Transfer to a wire rack and dust lightly with icing sugar or cocoa powder, if desired. Serve warm or cold.

NOTE: Unlike small sponge cakes, the muffin mixture should virtually fill the cases before cooking to achieve the traditional shape.

VARIATIONS

Add 5 ml (1 tsp) ground cinnamon or mixed spice when sifting together the dry ingredients.

TECHNIQUE

Spoon the muffin mixture into the paper cases, piling it up slightly in the centres.

SYRUPY SEMOLINA HALVA

Grainy semolina, baked to form a firm sponge base for citrus fruits saturated in spicy syrup, evokes the flavour of near eastern patisserie! Allow the sponge to steep for several hours or overnight in the thick syrup so that the syrup is thoroughly absorbed. Serve accompanied by thick yogurt and strong black coffee.

MAKES 10 SLICES

125 g (4 oz) unsalted butter,
  softened
125 g (4 oz) light muscovado
  sugar
grated rind of 1 orange
grated rind of 1 lemon
30 ml (2 tbsp) lemon juice
2 eggs
175 g (6 oz) semolina
5 ml (1 tsp) baking powder
125 g (4 oz) ground almonds
30 ml (2 tbsp) poppy seeds
TO FINISH
2 oranges
2 lemons
300 g (10 oz) caster sugar
300 ml (½ pint) freshly
  squeezed orange juice
2 cinnamon sticks, halved

PREPARATION TIME
30 minutes
COOKING TIME
30 minutes
FREEZING
Suitable: Cake only

485 CALS PER SLICE

1. Preheat the oven to 220°C (425°F) Mark 7. Grease and base-line a shallow 23 cm (9 inch) square baking tin. Cream the butter and sugar together until pale and fluffy.

2. Add the orange and lemon rind, lemon juice, eggs, semolina, baking powder, ground almonds and poppy seeds. Beat well until evenly mixed, then turn into the prepared tin and level the surface. Bake for about 20 minutes until slightly risen and turning golden. Remove from the oven and leave to cool in the tin. Peel off the paper, then return to the tin.

3. To finish, finely pare the rind from 1 orange and 1 lemon in strips using a citrus zester. Cut away all the white pith from both oranges and lemons, then thinly slice the fruit. Place the sugar in a heavy-based saucepan with the orange juice, cinnamon sticks and pared fruit rind. Heat gently, stirring until the sugar dissolves, then bring to the boil and boil for 3 minutes.

4. Remove the pared fruit rind and cinnamon from the syrup with a slotted spoon and reserve. Pour just over half of the syrup evenly over the surface of the cake. Scatter the fruit slices, pared rind and cinnamon sticks on top.

5. Return the remaining syrup to the heat and cook for another 5 minutes

or until thickened and beginning to caramelise. Pour evenly over the fruit and leave for several hours before cutting. Store in an airtight plastic container for up to 4-5 days.

NOTE: If preferred, you can arrange the decorative fruits in lines to make cutting easier.

TECHNIQUE

Beat the cake ingredients together until thoroughly mixed; the consistency will be fairly thick.

CHOCOLATE LEAF GÂTEAU

For this stunning gâteau a light, chocolate genoese is split and generously filled with a white chocolate and Cointreau-flavoured cream, then topped with a glossy dark chocolate cream icing and crowned with chocolate leaves. Use a variety of well-defined leaves to make the decoration – for optimum effect.

MAKES 14 SLICES

50 g (2 oz) unsalted butter
5 eggs
150 g (5 oz) caster sugar
125 g (4 oz) plain white flour
25 g (1 oz) cocoa powder
FILLING
200 g (7 oz) white chocolate
300 ml (½ pint) double
 cream
75 ml (5 tbsp) Cointreau or
 other orange-flavoured
 liqueur
ICING
225 g (8 oz) plain dark
 chocolate, in pieces
225 g (8 oz) double cream
TO DECORATE
75 g (3 oz) bitter chocolate
75 g (3 oz) plain dark
 chocolate
75 g (3 oz) milk chocolate
selection of clean, dry
 leaves, such as rose, large
 mint, lemon geranium
 and small bay leaves

PREPARATION TIME
1½ hours, plus cooling
COOKING TIME
30 minutes
FREEZING
Suitable: Before icing

560 CALS PER SLICE

1. Preheat the oven to 180°C (350°F) Mark 4. Grease and line a 23 cm (9 inch) spring-release cake tin. Melt the butter in a saucepan; leave to cool slightly.

2. Put the eggs and sugar in a large heat-proof bowl standing over a pan of hot water. Whisk until pale and creamy, and thick enough to leave a trail on the surface when the whisk is lifted.

3. Remove from the heat and whisk until cool. Sift together the flour and cocoa powder, then fold half into the egg mixture using a metal spoon. Pour the butter around the edge of the mixture and lightly fold in. Gradually fold in the remaining flour and cocoa.

4. Pour into the tin. Bake for about 30 minutes until well risen, just firm to touch and beginning to shrink from sides of tin. Turn out and cool on a wire rack.

5. To make the filling, finely grate the white chocolate. Whip cream with the liqueur until thickened but not peaking. Fold in the chocolate. Split the sponge horizontally and sandwich together with the cream. Invert onto a wire rack so that the flat base is now the top.

6. For the icing, place the chocolate in a heavy-based saucepan with the cream. Heat gently until chocolate is almost melted. Remove from heat and stir until smooth and glossy; let cool slightly.

7. Position a large plate or tray under the wire rack holding the cake. Pour the icing onto the cake. Using a palette knife, ease the icing down the side until the cake is completely covered. Carefully transfer to a serving plate.

8. For the chocolate leaves, break up the bitter chocolate and place in a heat-proof bowl over a pan of hot water and leave until melted. Repeat with the plain and milk chocolate; keep separate.

9. Using a paintbrush, paint the under-sides of the leaves with the different melted chocolates, taking it just to the edges. (You'll need about 15 of each shade). Leave in a cool place or refrigerate until set. Carefully peel the leaves away from the chocolate. Press the chocolate leaves gently around the sides of the gâteau to decorate.

TECHNIQUE

Once all of the icing has been poured over the top of the cake, ease it down the side, spreading with a palette knife.

COCONUT GÂTEAU WITH LIME AND KIRSCH

This beautiful white sponge is made using a meringue base into which the dry ingredients and flavourings are folded. Lime zest speckles the sponge and a kirsch syrup gives a moist kick. Freshly toasted coconut shavings and syrupy lime slices add both sweetness and tang to the rich cream coating.

MAKES 10-12 SLICES

7 egg whites

good pinch of salt

5 ml (1 tsp) cream of tartar

10 ml (2 tsp) vanilla essence

300 g (10 oz) caster sugar

finely grated rind of 2 limes

50 g (2 oz) freshly grated
   coconut, or desiccated
   coconut

125 g (4 oz) plain white flour

TO ASSEMBLE

4 limes

50 g (2 oz) caster sugar

60 ml (4 tbsp) kirsch

125 g (4 oz) piece fresh
   coconut, or coconut
   shreds

450 ml (¾ pint) double
   cream

45 ml (3 tbsp) icing sugar

175 g (6 oz) Greek-style
   yogurt

PREPARATION TIME
45 minutes, plus cooling
COOKING TIME
30 minutes
FREEZING
Suitable: Cake only

515-430 CALS PER SLICE

1. Preheat the oven to 160°C (325°F) Mark 3. Grease and base-line two 20 cm (8 inch) sandwich tins. Whisk the egg whites in a large bowl until just holding their shape. Add the salt and cream of tartar and whisk until stiff but not dry. Gradually whisk in the sugar, a little at a time, whisking well between each addition until stiff and very shiny. Whisk in the lime rind with the last of the sugar.

2. Add the coconut, then sift in the flour and lightly fold in until just incorporated. Divide between the tins and level the surfaces. Bake for 30 minutes until the surfaces are pale golden and crusty. Leave to cool in the tins.

3. For the decoration, finely pare the rind from two of the limes in shreds, using a sharp knife. Remove the peel and white pith from all 4 limes; thinly slice the flesh. Dissolve the sugar in 150 ml (¼ pint) water in a small heavy-based pan over a low heat. Add the lime slices and shredded rind and cook gently for 1 minute. Drain with a slotted spoon and reserve. Leave the syrup to cool.

4. Stir the kirsch into the cooled syrup. Split each cake in half horizontally and drizzle each layer with the syrup. If using fresh coconut, cut away the skin, then pare the flesh using a swivel vegetable peeler. Lightly toast the parings or coconut shreds until turning golden.

5. Whip the cream with the icing sugar until just peaking, then fold in the yogurt. Place one cake layer on a serving plate and spread with a little of the cream mixture. Arrange a quarter of the lime slices on top and sprinkle with a little of the coconut shavings. Repeat the layers twice, using up half the cream and most of the coconut and lime slices. Top with the final cake layer.

6. Spread the remaining cream all over the cake. Decorate the top with the remaining lime slices and coconut, and the pared lime rind. Chill in the refrigerator until ready to serve.

TECHNIQUE

Using a metal tablespoon, carefully fold the flour and coconut into the meringue mixture until just incorporated.

HAZELNUT MERINGUE GÂTEAU

Tiers of lightly spiced meringue – laced with two-tone chocolate pieces – form a delicious case for lightly whipped cream and a hazelnut praline. For a lighter gâteau, replace half of the cream with thick Greek-style yogurt or fromage frais. You can also increase the amount of spice if you prefer a more intense flavour.

MAKES 10 SLICES

MERINGUE
125 g (4 oz) shelled
   hazelnuts
5 egg whites
250 g (9 oz) caster sugar
2.5 cm (½ tsp) ground mixed
   spice
75 g (3 oz) white chocolate
   chopped
75 g (3 oz) plain chocolate,
   chopped
TO ASSEMBLE
75 g (3 oz) shelled hazelnuts
125 g (4 oz) caster sugar
300 ml (½ pint) double
   cream
cocoa powder, for dusting

PREPARATION TIME
40 minutes, plus cooling
COOKING TIME
About 1½ hours
FREEZING
Not suitable

630 CALS PER SLICE

1. Line 2 baking sheets with non-sticking baking parchment. Draw a 23 cm (9 inch) circle onto one sheet, using a plate as a guide. On the other sheet, draw a 17.5 cm (6½ inch) circle. Turn the paper over. Preheat the oven to 140°C (275°F) Mark 1.

2. To make the meringue, lightly toast the hazelnuts, then chop roughly. Whisk the egg whites in a bowl until stiff but not dry. Gradually whisk in the sugar, a tablespoon at a time, whisking well between each addition until the meringue is stiff and very shiny. Whisk in the spice with the last of the sugar. Carefully fold in the chopped hazelnuts and white and plain chocolate.

3. Spoon the meringue onto the circles, then spread neatly into rounds. Bake for about 1½ hours until dry and the undersides are firm when tapped. Turn the oven off and leave the meringues to cool in the oven.

4. For the praline, lightly oil a baking sheet. Put the hazelnuts in a small heavy-based pan with the sugar. Place over a gentle heat, stirring until the sugar melts. Continue cooking until the mixture caramelises to a rich golden brown colour, then pour onto the baking sheet. Leave to cool and harden.

5. Place the praline in a polythene bag and beat with a rolling pin until very coarsely crushed.

6. Carefully transfer the largest meringue round to a serving plate. Whip the cream until softly peaking, then spread over the meringue. Scatter with the praline. Cover with the smaller meringue round and dust the top of the gâteau with cocoa powder.

NOTE: Remember to switch the baking sheets around halfway through cooking the meringue rounds, to ensure an even result.

TECHNIQUE

Spread the hazelnut meringue onto the prepared baking sheets, just to the edges of the marked circles. Swirl the edges of the large meringue and the whole surface of the smaller meringue with a palette knife.

GINGERBREAD NATIVITY

This spicy gingerbread stable with its simple figures is easier to make than it looks – especially if you follow the step-by-step guide (overleaf) and use the template outlines provided. If it seems like too much work, try making tree decorations instead. Simply stamp out stars, trees etc, using suitable cutters and make a small hole in the top of each one – to enable a ribbon to be threaded through after baking, for hanging on the tree.

MAKES I NATIVITY

350 g (12 oz) plain white
    flour
5 ml (I tsp) bicarbonate of
    soda
30 ml (2 tbsp) ground ginger
15 ml (I tbsp) ground
    cinnamon
2.5 ml (½ tsp) ground cloves
125 g (4 oz) butter
175 g (6 oz) soft light brown
    sugar
60 ml (2 tbsp) golden syrup
I egg (size 4)
CARAMEL
125 g (4 oz) caster sugar
30 ml (2 tbsp) water
TO DECORATE
twiglets or lean straw
    matting
demerara and/or other
    brown sugars, for
    sprinkling
a little glacé or royal icing
food colourings
edible gold leaf or lustre
    powder
few toffees or flat sweets

PREPARATION TIME
About 2 hours, plus drying
COOKING TIME
8-10 minutes
FREEZING
Suitable: Uncooked gingerbread
dough only

I. Cut out templates for the stable (see pages 186-7). Line two baking sheets with non-stick baking parchment. Preheat the oven to 190°C (375°F) Mark 5.

2. Sift the flour with the bicarbonate of soda and spices into a large bowl. Rub in the butter until the mixture resembles fine breadcrumbs. Stir in the sugar.

3. Warm the syrup very slightly and beat in the egg. Cool slightly, then pour onto the flour mixture. Beat with a wooden spoon to a soft dough. Bring together with your hands and knead until smooth. Cut off one third of the dough, wrap in cling film and reserve.

4. On a lightly floured surface, roll out the other piece of dough to a 5 mm (¼ inch) thickness. Using the stable templates and a sharp knife, cut out each shape. Carefully transfer to the baking sheets, straighten any edges and chill for 15 minutes. Knead the trimmings into the reserved dough, re-wrap and chill to make the figures later.

5. Bake the stable pieces for 8-10 minutes or until golden brown. Leave to cool and harden for 10 minutes on the baking sheet, then transfer to a wire rack to cool completely.

6. To make the caramel, dissolve the sugar in the water in a heavy-based pan

over a low heat, then boil to a pale caramel. Immediately dip the base of the pan in cool water to stop further cooking. Use this caramel to join the edges of the stable together and to cement it to a cake board. Join the roof to the stable. Stick twiglets or straw matting to the roof, if liked. Sprinkle sugar(s) in and around the stable.

7. Using the templates (on pages 188-9), cut out the figures and carefully place on the baking sheets. Bake as before, checking after 8 minutes. Cool as before (use any remaining dough to make biscuits).

8. Decorate the figures with gold leaf or lustre powder, and coloured glacé or royal icing. Allow to dry before assembling around the stable. Use a toffee or sweet and a little icing to cement the base of each figure to the board.

TECHNIQUE

To make the caramel, cook the sugar syrup to a pale golden colour.

GINGERBREAD NATIVITY

The gingerbread nativity is fun to make – especially if you have children to help you! The following step-by-step guide shows you how to make and assemble the stable, and how to decorate the figures. Use edible decorations, unless you make it known that the nativity is not to be eaten.

1. Cut out templates for the stable (see right), using greaseproof paper or cardboard. Line two baking sheets with non-stick baking parchment.

2. Roll out the larger piece of gingerbread dough to a 5 mm (¼ inch) thickness. Using the templates and a sharp knife, cut out one of each shape.

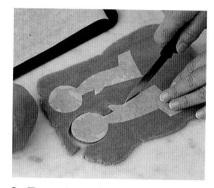

3. Trace the outlines of the figures (overleaf) to make templates for Mary, Joseph, Baby Jesus, Angel Gabriel, Star of Bethlehem, Kings and Shepherds. Roll out the remaining dough and place the templates on the dough. Cut out using a sharp knife. Remember to cut 3 kings and 2-3 shepherds.

4. Carefully transfer the shapes to the baking sheets without destroying the shapes. Straighten any edges and chill for 15 minutes.

5. Bake the pieces of gingerbread in a preheated oven at 190°C (375°F) Mark 5 for 8-10 minutes or until golden brown. Leave on the baking sheet for 10 minutes, then transfer to a wire rack to cool completely.

6. Use the caramel to join the edges of the stable together and to cement it to a covered cake board. Dip the edges in the caramel and push them together or use a spoon to coat the edges. Remelt the caramel as necessary by sitting the pan in a saucepan of boiling water until it liquifies again. Join the roof to the stable with the caramel.

7. Stick twiglets or clean straw matting to the roof, or leave plain if preferred. Scatter different shades of sugar around the stable to resemble sand and earth.

9. Decorate the characters with glacé or royal icing. Allow to dry before assembling in and around the stable.

10. Cement a toffee or flat sweet to the base of each figure with a little icing or caramel so that it will stand upright. Stick suitable sweets onto the Kings to resemble their gifts.

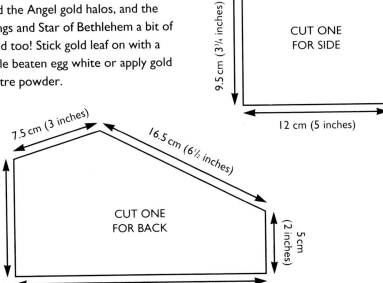

8. Give Baby Jesus, Mary, Joseph and the Angel gold halos, and the Kings and Star of Bethlehem a bit of gold too! Stick gold leaf on with a little beaten egg white or apply gold lustre powder.

STABLE TEMPLATES

CUT ONE FOR SIDE
5 cm (2 inches)
12 cm (5 inches)

CUT ONE FOR SIDE
9.5 cm (3¾ inches)
12 cm (5 inches)

CUT ONE FOR ROOF
18 cm (7 inches)
13.5 cm (5½ inches) including overhang

7.5 cm (3 inches)
16.5 cm (6½ inches)
9.5 cm (3¾ inches)
CUT ONE FOR BACK
5 cm (2 inches)
20.5 cm (8¼ inches)

CUT ONE FOR ROOF
9 cm (3½ inches) including overhang
13.5 cm (5½ inches) including overhang

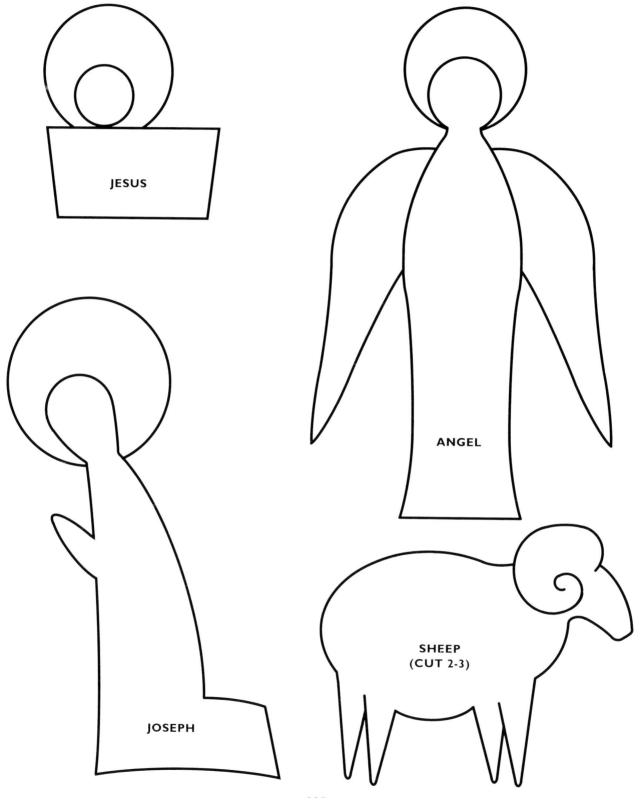

JESUS

ANGEL

JOSEPH

SHEEP
(CUT 2-3)

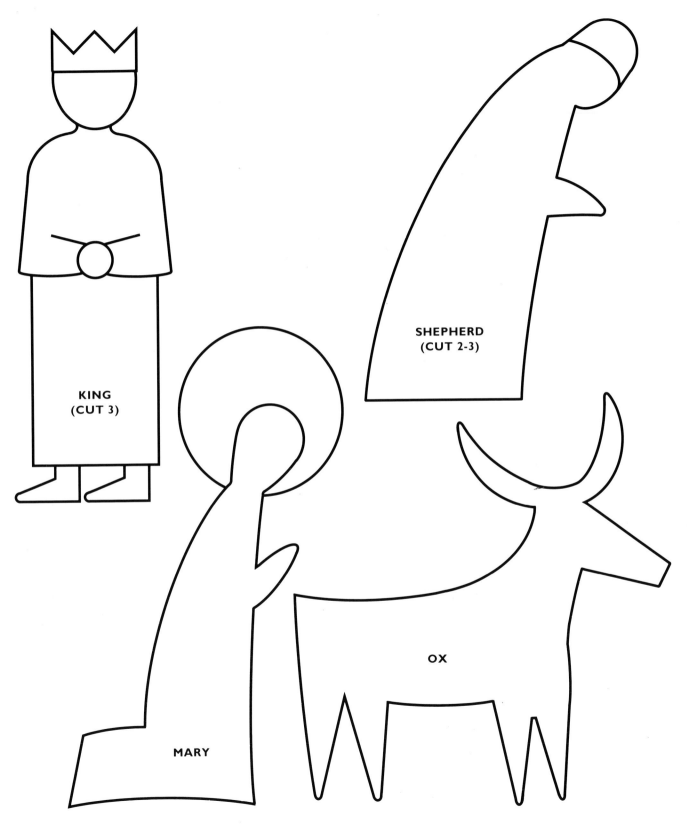

KING
(CUT 3)

SHEPHERD
(CUT 2-3)

MARY

OX